Prologue

Most war stories tell about troop movements and areas conquered; usually giving statistics about how many soldiers killed on either side. It is difficult for historians to evaluate the feelings and aspirations of the individual soldier. In my narrative, I have tried to get behind the statistics and capture the feelings and horrors of the men who determine the outcome of the battles.

When someone says 200 or 500, or any gross number of casualties, I think of each individual in his death throes, and what his loss means to his family. His death is final. He is no more; the fact that they could not be near makes this more poignant. His family could neither comfort him in his last moments, nor bury him and have the cleansing event of a final farewell.

Every time I saw a dead soldier I would try to place him in a family, imagining the grief the cold telegram would bring them. I am sure it was difficult to realize that this brother or son was no more. To hear about this loss through a telegram had to be quite abstract, but no less painful, when he was already so far away. They could only guess at his state of mind in his last moments. At the same time I tried to surmise what the combat soldier thought his loss would mean to his family, when the going got tough and he knew he had a good chance of not surviving. I'm sure that every soldier locked in combat, seeing death all around him, had to think of what his death would mean to someone back home especially as he read a letter from home. These letters gave one a small sense of reality to balance the day to day living in this unreal world.

This is not a chronological recitation of battles, or advances made in the field; there are many accounts of troop movements and engagements with the enemy forces written by a vast number of other writers. This document does not tell what Company, Regiment, Corps, or Army unit was engaged in this conflict — but rather my personal feelings and horrors left over from this war that I am trying to project.

I was privileged to have a small part in this intense and historic event. Being part of battalion headquarters company, I occasionally had the opportunity to be involved in dangerous but dramatic events. I infrequently toured the front lines, which kept me from being constantly involved in dangerous situations. Because I was not traumatized by the horror of combat, it is probably easier for me to write candidly about these events.

I hope to document my thoughts and feelings before they fade entirely. I will set down facts as I remember them almost fifty years later. It is just possible that someone might want to know what it felt like in that unreal world. Each man involved in combat living responds individually to his own unique experiences. To one soldier, the noise and confusion may be overwhelming; to another, being shot at or shelled could be his most horrible memory, to someone else, the filth and clutter of being surrounded by bombed out buildings and blown up vehicles might be his worst recollection. Every soldier has his own nightmare left over from the war.

I especially remember the dirt and disorder in partly-destroyed homes, and we would bivouac in them. They usually had a succession of people living in them temporarily before we occupied them. No one had the time or inclination to clean anything, so filth and garbage were placed in layers in these temporary shelters as time went on. Sometimes your shelter was an abandoned German fox hole or bunker. They had occupied these holes for weeks or months before we found them; so you can imagine the amount of clutter and garbage that would accumulate when cleanliness was way down on their list of priorities.

So you can see that my most vivid recollection of the war, was the filth and clutter from the destruction all about me — not necessarily the danger from being shelled or fired upon.

My aversion to filth and clutter does not diminish my thoughts about the brave men that I lived with, talked to and exchanged fears and frustrations with. My thoughts did not keep me from feeling the individual horrors the soldiers who were maimed or killed at the brink of death. I also would like to think that my description of battle zones provides some insight into what a forest looks like after intense shelling, or the debris from destroyed buildings and military equipment and their impact on the soldiers.

Have you ever wondered how they can take an ordinary lad with a family that loves him, has all the aspirations of youth, possibly a girlfriend, and put him into a uniform and train him to advance against an enemy trying desperately to kill him? He sees his comrades around him falling, one of them is shot through the face, the noise of battle engulfs him and

Notes of a Private Soldier

AN AMERICAN G.I. IN EUROPE
1944-1945

Harold Knittel

Notes of a Private Soldier

Copyright © 1993 by Harold Knittel

Harold W. Knittel 5b 3 -2 66--72 78
1560 N Locust St.
Canby, OR 97013-3156

Cover and book design by Ashley Fletcher

ISBN 0-9672883-0-4

Printed and bound in the United States of America

shuts out the rest of the world. He is frightened to death, virtually paralyzed by the enormity of the things that are happening around him; but still responding to his orders to move forward to a certain objective and kill any enemy that stands between this objective and him.

Killing humans is not a normal reaction for any human being. This killing mentality stems from the necessity to preserve his own life, and is made more acceptable by his horrible living condition; making any semblance of "normal" so far into his past that he is acting out of just basic instincts as though he is in another world. This world is so remote from the life he was brought up in that I'm sure he does not think of or try to correlate this former life with all the horrible things going on around him now. This world was thrust on him in stages as his combat living progressed in ever changing and deteriorating conditions. Just the very surroundings and living conditions of the combat infantryman are horrifying; sleeping in a muddy hole in the ground, constantly being shelled by the enemy, eating cold food and being dirty and wet most of the time. His clothes are heavy with mud and water. You have to force yourself to take off your shoes and rub your feet to get circulation back into them or you will suffer the malady of trench feet. This condition is brought on by having your feet constantly wet, they seem to swell up in your shoes and gradually lose feeling and finally the circulation slows to where it becomes so dangerous that you could lose your toes or parts of your foot. This problem and other seemingly minor difficulties are forced into the background by the constant danger from enemy shelling.

I have this theory that most successful units in combat are those that are kept in constant contact with the enemy. If you have any lengthy respite from this hell it is harder to accept any new assignment that brings you in contact with the enemy. This theory is reinforced by the fact that most of the "shell shock," or combat fatigue cases occur in individuals that were wounded and sent to the rear for recovery, then returned to front line duty. The dry, clean beds and decent food, plus the lack of immediate danger during the hospital stay makes it almost impossible for some soldiers to face the rigors of combat again. Many "flip out" or go into shell shock to mentally escape this impossible way of life. Most of their daily experiences, prior to being "mercifully" wounded consisted of hunkering down in a muddy hole with the rain soaking their bedding, dreaming of just one night in a warm dry bed. All this time, mortars, rockets and artillery raining death down.

Just a few short months before, they were coming ashore in a landing craft, with artillery shells hitting the water all around them. When they got close enough to shore the front of the landing craft dropped down a ramp; exposing all the men in the craft to a hail of mortar and machine gun fire. They move forward against this torrent of flying metal; scared beyond reason, nerves taught, sure that the next bullet is ready to impact one of them. They see their buddies that they've been living with during training being hit and going down; crying out for the medics, God or anyone that can help them. These are not abstract human beings they met on the street; these are boys they have been sharing their lives with. They by now know each other intimately, their very hopes and aspirations; they have shared letters from home and are somehow intimately involved in each others families. As their buddies go down they may even try to imagine what this terrible wounding or death may have on family members of these fallen men. It all seems to be such a waste of life, but their training impels them to go forward; possibly influenced by an indoctrinating speech conferred on them in training camp "if you are wounded you will go to the rear and be treated, if you are not killed or wounded you just were concerned over nothing."

We all have seen some of these landings on T.V., the men being hit and falling down like ducks in a shooting gallery. These are not ducks; these are living, breathing human beings that are still hoping to beat the odds and still live another day. They are horrified at seeing their buddies hit and falling; this amplifies their fear and feeling of vulnerability, they are sure their turn is next. It may be a bunk mate or a boy they have shared letters or a box of goodies from home with.

Accepting all this as "normal" stems mostly from their harsh basic training in infantry tactics. This training is meant to be difficult enough to prepare one for the realities of actual combat.

Off the Farm

L ike thousands of other young men plodding through uneventful lives in Depression-era America, my desire was to leave the farm and "join the Navy and see the world."

Having completed high school with average grades, and knowing I would never be able to afford college, any escape to adventure seemed preferable to a life of drudgery on the family farm in South Dakota.

Yet, despite my romantic longings for the life of a "jolly tar at sea," I was a typical country kid, a bumpkin who had no idea of how to sign up for military service, let alone money enough to travel to the recruiting office, which, like the ocean, was many miles away.

So for the next three years I just plodded along, taking care of my mother's farm with hopes that someday my fortunes would change.

In August of 1940, they did. Uncle Sam plucked me for the Draft. World War II had been going hot and heavy in Europe for nearly a year by this time, and though America was still neutral, we knew that our getting involved would be only a matter of time.

My local draft board, all of them friends, told me I was eligible for a full deferment since farming was an essential service. But I wanted to get out of there and I didn't care if it meant going into the Army or off to a shooting war. At least I'd be free to travel and would see another part of the world.

Having received an extension, I quickly disposed of the farm and its livestock and machinery, and soon

AUTHOR AND MOTHER AT FARM
IN SOUTH DAKOTA

was on my way to the induction center. We traveled by train and for some reason I was put in charge of six Indian boys drafted from the Rosebud Indian Reservation, a group lubricated by whiskey and more than a handful on our long trip to Ft. Leavenworth, Kansas.

Fort Leavenworth was large military establishment bustling with activity as draftees poured in to fill the new barracks that were going up everywhere. My stay there was short. After testing and evaluation I was put back on a train with orders to report to an anti-aircraft training camp near San Diego, Calif.

The trip west was boring and uneventful, though after we reached the coast I was delighted to see my first big cities: San Francisco, Oakland, Los Angeles and other places that were new and exciting to a farm lad who had never been to a town with more than ten thousand people.

Our destination was Camp Callon, located at Torry Pines just north of San Diego. This was a large, well-organized military complex and I learned I would be trained in the use of anti-aircraft (A.A.) guns deployed in units of the U.S. Coastal Artillery.

(I also quickly learned that A.A. duty was preferable to serving with the infantry — though, as it is in the Army, I would end up with the infantry three years later anyway.)

Our camp was on the ocean, ironically, and this was also a first for me since the only ocean I knew about had been on geography maps. Of course there was a reason for our being located beside the ocean. As part of the coastal artillery, we practiced firing at targets towed by airplanes over the water.

In those days, before California was overrun by people, this was a wonderful area to be stationed. We were close to Bing Crosby's Del Mar Race Track, and we were a short distance from La Jolla, a beautiful and exclusive residential area whose palm tree-lined streets created an exotic environment, particularly for a South Dakota farm boy. San Diego was farther south and seemed an awesome metropolis, and on a three-day pass we might even travel north to the wonders of San Francisco.

Transportation was no problem for a serviceman in those days. All you had to do was stick out your thumb and you had a ride. We learned rather quickly to take advantage of the great California hospitality. Although there were hundreds of thousands of servicemen in the area, the civilians treated us like kings. On Sundays they would even drive out to our post and invite us home to dinner.

But then, on another Sunday, Dec. 7, 1941, our comfortable world collapsed and we began to earn our pay.

I had just finished three months basic training and was sitting in the barracks, my bags packed for a long-awaited furlough, when the news came over the radio. Furloughs were canceled and we were put on extreme alert, issued live ammunition and steel helmets and, in those days before radar, ordered to man listening posts to monitor for Japanese planes that everyone believed would soon attack.

After a week, however, when things calmed down, we were sent to join the 217th Anti-aircraft battery stationed near Oakland on San Francisco Bay. This was a National Guard unit from Northern Minnesota, a bunch of "weekend warriors" who were extremely unhappy over being called to active duty. Typical of closely knit National Guard units, the commanding officer was postmaster in one of the communities, while the officers were assorted businessmen and town officials. They weren't too receptive to outsiders like myself joining their unit, making it a rather dismal two and a half years I spent with them.

During this time our responsibility was guarding the San Francisco Bay area. Our duties involved manning searchlights and gun emplacements in most of the outlying areas, as well as on an old shaky wooden pier that extended for seven miles out into the bay. No one liked to go out there, for obvious reasons, and even in the summertime the nights were so cold we had to wear woolen long-johns and heavy coats.

(Years later, remembering nights shivering on that pier, I would concur with Mark Twain's observation that the coldest winter he'd ever spent was a summer in San Francisco.)

Not only was it cold, but, as you might expect, on Sunday's the rickety old pier was crowded with fishermen who often left trash fish on the pier to rot. By Tuesday the smell could be unbearable.

One of our better positions was out on Skyline Drive in the foothills of Oakland, an ideal trysting spot for lovers. Issued with night vision binoculars, we would prowl the area for "suspicious" cars and after informing them that this was a military installation, run them off.

Of course they would be very unhappy with us, especially when we caught them with their pants down, but it made a boring job enjoyable. Once we caught a sailor in a vulnerable position, and when we told he was parked in a restricted zone he became quite abusive, which was completely understandable since he was at a critical moment in his backseat relationship.

Since we had no great love for sailors, probably out of envy, we forced him to move on despite his pleas for "just a few minutes more." He grumbled and swore as he pulled up his bell-bottom trousers, and I told him that next time he might have better luck if he treated the Army with a little more respect.

On weekends the road was part of an equestrian trail, and we made some acquaintances among the horse people. Being from South Dakota, and accustomed to farm animals, I quickly made friends (and some liaisons) with the riders, and discovered that many of the horse people were as lonely as we were. We were stretching the rules a bit, but it worked out quite nicely for all of us.

About this time I came down with a case of appendicitis and was taken to Letterman General Hospital. On the way to the hospital the ambulance picked up a hitchhiking soldier. When I commented on this, and the fact that the ambulance had no siren to speed it up in traffic, the driver said they were able to stabilize most patients. This gave them time to get to a hospital without hurrying. He said my appendix would be packed in ice and probably not operated on until Wednesday when they did their usual "flow of appendectomies."

As it turned out, my appendix was about to burst, so I was operated on that night.

After surgery I was put on a ward with 200 other "appendectomies." To the average "Joe" like me, it seemed as if we were victims of an epidemic. But when dealing with more than a million servicemen in the Bay Area, 200 did not warrant epidemic proportions.

After field duty, it felt good to take it easy for a while. During recovery I was sent over to Ft. Mason on San Francisco Bay where I was given no duty until being returned to my company.

When I returned, my company was undergoing a welcome transformation; many of the old National Guard officers were being retired and replaced by officers of the Regular Army. With this change, we began to get a taste of West Point discipline, which I appreciated since the company was being run more smoothly.

Instead of lying around feeling sorry for ourselves, we were placed on a strict exercise routine and our duties became more rigidly defined. For the first time we began to feel like we were part of an Army being trained for war, and morale improved considerably. I was proud to be part of an Army that was disciplined and trained to fight. Though I had been drafted, I still craved adventure.

Before long things began to change dramatically. Our old companies were broken up and new companies were formed, and I was sent to another unit commanded by a West Point captain whose first name I can't remember, but whose last name was "Smith."

He was a fine officer and I was relieved that few of the original National Guard men had moved with me. I was selected as company clerk and supply sergeant "without the rating or pay," and most of us were doing double-duty as it was a small, under-strengthed company.

My relationship with Captain Smith was quite good. When we went overseas, he was instrumental in my being assigned to a position at battalion headquarters in an infantry regiment, claiming my M.O. (military occupation) was that of a radio operator which probably saved my life when we got into combat, since it was a much safer occupation than that of a rifleman in a line company.

CHAPTER TWO

Moving Toward War

After three years in the Coast Artillery, defending the San Francisco Bay area from the Japanese Imperial Air Force, I was transferred to an infantry training camp in Texas, to be trained in "infantry basics."

This meant I would soon be replacing a soldier on the front lines, provoking the question: What happened to the soldier I am going to replace? Not a happy thought.

Now, however, after months of living in disorganized limbo, we at least knew what we were going to do: kill or be killed, and neither was on our list of priorities.

The troop train was an ancient and miserable conveyance that was hot, crowded and the coal burning engine assaulted us with soot and flying cinders. We were certainly not "priority baggage," and we spent a large part of the trip sitting on sidings while more important freight went by.

It took us a week to get from San Francisco to our destination, Camp Maxie in Texas. Three of those days were spent just getting across Texas, which was hot, flat, desolate and as large as many small countries.

Infantry training camps are located in places selected for their harsh environment, and Camp Maxie, in Northern Texas, was certainly suited to our harsh, despotic training. The weather in summer was extremely hot, and if it did rain the air became sticky and humid. The barracks had no eaves so it if rained we had to shut the windows and the air was steamy and stifling. The mess halls were so hot heat waves rippled through the air.

Outside the parade ground was a glaring white sandy soil that could almost make you snow-blind from the sun glare. Crawling around in the stuff filled our sweaty clothes with grit that was hell to get out before inspection, which was held each evening just before chow.

The training cadre seemed cruel beyond belief, and the penalty for the slightest infraction could mean marching endlessly around the parade ground with full field pack, helmet and rifle. Punishment was entirely up to the training corporal and sergeant, and I managed to receive the full ire of sergeant after I made a derogatory remark about his hometown baseball team.

From then on I was a marked man. He went as far as to march backwards in front of me to make sure my eyes were straight forward, for to let your eyes stray was an infraction. He singled me out during inspections, purposely making me nervous by needlessly examining my clothes and equipment with a fine tooth comb.

Yet, though he had it in for me, he never gigged me or failed me at any inspection. He was a good enough soldier to respect my extra effort, though it was almost impossible to swallow my pride and not let him discover the slightest weakness in my character.

Later, however, I would realize, like so many others, that he was doing me a favor, the harsh discipline a factor in transforming me from a lackadaisical Coast Artilleryman into a soldier whose well-honed infantryman's skills would help me survive overseas.

I learned to separate my feelings from my discomforts, and when I got overseas I realized how this hard-learned personal detachment, the instinctive ability to react more as machine than man, could save you from cracking up in the violence of combat.

I was a tough kid anyway, raised on a farm and used to long hours and hard work. I could endure the forced marches, sometimes fifteen miles at a time, and most other physical hardships. The chiggers, however, were a different matter. Texas chiggers were extremely rapacious, bigger and more vicious, and on night exercises would burrow under our skins and cause terrible itching.

Yet these planned and unplanned obstacles only made us physically and psychologically tougher. It is possible to condition most people to accept unnatural or dangerous conditions with the proper training and environment if done in proper stages and with proper procedures, i.e., training a man to jump from an airplane into enemy territory.

At Camp Maxie, I knew that most of us who had been languishing in the Coastal Artillery would have quickly fallen apart in combat. The number of men from our outfit who would have succumbed to combat fatigue or "shell shock" would have been much greater without the baptism of fire and harsh treatment we received in infantry training. At the obstacle course, we had to crawl between shell craters and barbed wire with machine guns firing over and around us. If you learned anything, you learned to not stick your butt in the air.

Ironically, I would learn that active combat seemed to affect most soldiers, who in time seemed numb to the unbelievable chaos around them. These men became noticeably subdued and quietly thoughtful; as if combat demanded a civilized response to its undisciplined fury.

At the completion of our training we were all given ten-day furloughs. When we returned from our furloughs, we found out that some of the more sadistic members of the training cadre were not there to greet our return. The only ones that stayed on were the ones who hadn't treated us badly. This was a good maneuver on the part of the officers in charge as some of the men that were treated very badly would have liked to retaliate. They would have had no reservation to beating up some of those tyrants, as our next assignment (combat) would have been about the same as going to the guard house.

We were all made believers of guard house discipline while still in the Coast Artillery. We were assigned 24-hour company guard duty at a prison stockade. This is an experience given to green troops to demonstrate that prison is much worse than combat.

There was a Major in charge of our detail who singled out a Native American boy to show us how bad things can be in a stockade. That day, at inspection he found a cigarette in the boy's pocket. After taking the cigarette he slammed his fist into the boy's gut, doubling him over.

Later, when he had the prisoners lined up for inspection, he had us surround the formation with rifles and bayonets. The Major circled around the Indian boy several times, then he called him out from the ranks to stand in front of his group of prisoners.

He then assigned one of us to get behind him, telling him to double time around the perimeter with one of us right behind him, our bayonet almost stabbing him in the rear. Every time he completed a lap he assigned a fresh guard to chase him. After he completed 10 laps (which was about 5 miles), he called him back into formation and made him stand at attention. He then circled around him, slapping him with his leather gloves if he moved at all. I do not know how the boy's heart could take that much inaction without rest. He was shaking from exhaustion so he couldn't stand perfectly still.

The Major called him to the front of the ranks once more to repeat the process again. When he called for one of us to repeat the gruesome experiment, this time not one man but the whole company stepped forward with our bayonets leveled at the Major's behind. Evidently he was scared enough of such a group reaction that he called off the experiment and dismissed us all. We never received any disciplinary action from this incident, so we figured the Major knew he was out of bounds. Today, that Major would have been court-martialed. We were all happy that in one hour we were relieved of this guard duty, and returned to our barracks quite satisfied.

This had happened when we were still in the Anti-aircraft unit of the Coast artillery, but we never forgot the horror that happened in that stockade.

Now we were trained as an infantry replacement package (cannon fodder) and we received our orders to the East Coast to be near our port of embarkation.

Finally we were going to war — And if there was any consolation, we would be fighting in Europe rather than the Orient, the Germans rather than the Japanese, this made us feel a lot better.

CHAPTER THREE

Shipping Out

A fter leaving Texas we were sent to Ft. Meade, Maryland, to be near our debarkation port in New Jersey. We were just a ragtag replacement package that had survived basic infantry training, and being in transit we were more of a disciplined mob than anything else.

We had no squads, platoons or companies, and our superiors did little more than herd us around and keep track of our numbers through a daily head count.

I had a buddy from Chicago, whose name I can't remember now, and after we observed this loose organization we started considering our options. We soon learned the number of people who could fit into our assigned barracks, and we also knew the number of men in our group. Through good old "guard house" reasoning we knew there would be a few bunks short and we slipped into a nearby casual barracks occupied by some small units who had no set routines.

A light went on in our outlaw brains. If we stayed back and ended up in that barracks we could be on our own. There was going to be a lot of vigorous training, including trips to the hated obstacle course, and with this in mind, we settled in.

The first morning we fell out with the group, we discovered there was no roll call, they just marched away to the training area. My buddy and I went with them to the first training exercise: an obstacle course realistically enhanced with live machine gun fire.

It looked dangerous as hell, but one of the training corporals assured us that only two men had been hit in the two years they had used the area, and both of them had survived.

My buddy and I looked at each other, and quickly decided we didn't like the odds. Hell, we were going to be shot at by Germans soon enough anyway. Slowly, so as not to draw attention, we dropped back until we were no longer part of the main group and sneaked back into the barracks, there to join a small group of others goofing off as well.

We soon became so creative and daring that we managed to avoid our main unit's training schedule together. In the mornings we would slip into Baltimore, the nearest city, but made sure we were back at camp by chow time. We were short of money to eat or do much else in town, but we also didn't want to get left behind if they shipped out without us. We wanted to go overseas with our unit — and we wanted to stay out of the guard house.

We'd return from a day in Baltimore and the rest of the unit would be recovering from a day at the obstacle course or a forced march, soaking their feet or bandaging blisters.

By shifting between barracks we had managed to become invisible, confusing our friends and the training cadre, who didn't know most of us from Adam anyway. We also spared ourselves a lot of hard work and blistered feet.

Being kind of a smartass anyway, I was very good at this sort of thing, having pulled a similar ploy back when a buddy and I were training in the Coast Artillery. We managed to enroll in a truck driver's training course to escape drill, registering for the course at platoon headquarters but not at the school, though we attended some of the classes. Mornings we would sneak off to the beach, returning in time for noon chow.

We kept this up for five weeks, attending about half the classes — usually those that involved actual driving of trucks — and at the end, still missing from the school's roster, managed to confuse a new training sergeant who issued us our GI drivers' licenses anyway.

When our training had been completed on the East Coast, our unit was formed into a "replacement package" (we called it "cannon fodder") and delivered aboard a troop ship for transportation to Europe.

Our ship was the *Isle de France*, which before the war was the third largest passenger ship in service. Though temporarily transformed into a vessel for hauling bulk human cargo, you could see it was a beautiful ship, with twelve-foot wide stairways and many luxurious appointments.

Unfortunately, traveling in "troop class" accommodations, like thousands of others, I remember most the long lines for chow, if you could call it that. There were two meals a day, and the British, who ran the ship, served the lousiest chow in the world despite the fact the food had been provided and paid for by the United States Army.

Meals were so bad that ships' stewards, who admitted the food was lousy, came around selling us sandwiches and cake made with our own food. But this lasted only a few days, until one of our officers made them knock it off, and ordered them to give us better food without paying for it.

By the time we crossed the Atlantic in 1944, the *Isle de France* was carrying 12,000 troops. On previous trips, the ship had transported 24,000 men, and I could only feel sorry for them since we spent most of our time jammed together, waiting in chow lines or trying to get into the bathrooms, which were impossibly scarce.

It took us seven days to arrive in Glasgow, Scotland. The ship was too large to bring into port, so we disembarked down large cargo nets into boats and barges that would take us ashore.

We were amazed to see the Scots scrubbing the streets after the fishing fleet had unloaded, but that's about all we saw of Scotland for there wasn't time to look around. We were quickly boarded onto tiny British railway cars for shipment to the English South Coast, there to be boarded on ships for the coast of Normandy.

Our first introduction to wartime living came as our train passed through Northern Scottish towns where children came out to wave at us. They had been separated from their parents and sent north to get way from the heavy bombing of English cities and industrial areas.

Ironically, the only British soil we stepped on was moving from our train to the ships in the English Channel. I have no knowledge about the size of our cross-channel boat, but we slept in hammocks, and, often hilariously, it took most of the night to learn to stay in them. One false move and over you went. And if you happened to reach out too far, you could spill out the next fellow, and the next, like a line of dominoes.

The next morning we were reintroduced to the dreadful British chow. Sausages, or "bangers," of mostly filler and a hint of meat. And the "coffee" I'll never forget. The British apparently don't drink much of it. They prepared it two or three gallons at a time with canned milk poured in ahead of time. The milk came to the top in an unappetizing scum, and with the bangers... Well, needless to say the K and C rations we had later on shore, though not great, were most welcome.

CHAPTER FOUR

Nearing the Front

T hree months after D-day we landed at Omaha Beach in Normandy. I was astounded at the destruction and waste all around us. This was my first glimpse of an actual combat zone and I could visualize the fury of the fighting that by now had moved inland across the French countryside.

The beach was still a dangerous place, as we soon found out. Several men were wounded when the heat of their campfire set off an undetected land mine. A short time later, there were more casualties after a truck ran over another mine. Looking around at the blasted German pillboxes, the shell holes, wire and other obstacles, I could imagine the hell it must have been on the day of the invasion.

Believe me, it is one thing to read about an event in a newspaper, but to see the aftermath firsthand makes your blood run cold. Loading into trucks to leave the beach area — and recalling the one that had just exploded — we felt the first real fear of what lay ahead.

Our conditioning would come gradually, as we neared the front, but as we moved inland we passed a huge allied cemetery covered with acres of crosses, while scattered about elsewhere were hastily dug German graves marked by their distinctive coal shuttle helmets and rifles. Evidently the Graves Registration company did not rebury the German casualties at this time.

As a naive South Dakota farm boy who had never been in a foreign country, I was intrigued by the sights around us. We passed through farming country, but it was a far cry from the vast, endless fields of the Plains where I grew up. The fields were small and tidy, and were bounded by trees and thick hedgerows that had provided tough defensive positions for the retreating German troops who used them in fierce holding actions.

The hedgerows were a tangle of heavy vines planted on low mounds that stretched endlessly, their tough, entwined roots hundreds of years old forming barriers that were nearly impregnable, even to the guns on our tanks.

The old French farm houses that were still standing were large stone or concrete buildings built onto the barns. Either the house was built on top of or attached directly to the end of the barn. Either way they smelled like the farm animals that occupied them. I was curious about the attached barns, and wondered if this arrangement was to protect the livestock from harm or outsiders, or to provide easy access in winter. Later, after noticing similar farm buildings in Belgium and Germany, I would learn that the animals' body heat provided extra warmth to the homes in cold weather.

The business buildings in the small towns were usually two or three stories tall with slate roofs and were built to last, as many had been in the same families for generations. In the States if a business building gets to be fifty years old, they tear it down and build a newer style of building. In Europe some of these business buildings are near a thousand years old and still being used.

Though I was moving toward the war, I was seeing the world, and it was a pleasant cultural experience to see how farmers lived in this part of France. The farms were clustered around small villages, and though the war had passed through here only months before, the farmers, who had experienced other wars, went about their daily chores and labors with fatalistic resignation. Being raised on a farm, I found their methods interesting. Since there were no tractors, the farming I saw was labor intensive, and they worked the small two- to ten-acre plots by hand, cutting their hay with scythes, raking it by hand and hauling it on small carts pulled by draft animals. Some times they had two horses to pull the hay wagon, often though they two cows, or even one horse and one cow. I suspected that their farm economy would not support two or even sometimes one nonproductive animal like horses. Actually this indicated that horses were a luxury, which they are usually are even in our country.

As we traveled across Northern France on our way to the front, we saw that the towns and cities had been mostly destroyed by the recent fighting, with the usual debris of war scattered along the shell-pocked roads and highways: burned-out trucks, tanks and other vehicles with a smell of death about them. The road signs were made of concrete, about three feet tall, and, ominously, resembled grave stones, with distances marked in kilometers instead of miles, so as we passed by them quickly I began to wonder how many kilometers it would be before we experienced our baptism of fire.

Our first night in France was spent in a bivouac set up in a woods that was peaceful and comfortable, a location that seemed almost planned to help us forget about the war. We were all young kids, part of a "replacement package," as they called it, and our leader, a first lieutenant, suggested a sing-along as a means of helping us forget for a while the horrors that we knew lay ahead.

There was one young kid, a Southern boy, who somehow, along with his other equipment, had managed to bring along a guitar. And since we were still quite some ways back from the front, we built a large bonfire and gathered around like Boy Scouts on a camp out.

I had never been a music lover, especially of the hillbilly kind, but the songs sung by the Southerner, who had a good voice and could really play, reminded us all of home and the evening turned out to be a satisfying experience. During our past weeks on the move about the only entertainment we'd had was lining up for chow. We gradually adjusted to a lifestyle that was as basic as it could be; soon we would not even have the necessities of life, like fire and shelter, not to mention safety from the constant presence of death.

Though we were bivouacked in the woods for only a few days, and savored most of it, we were never free of the anxiety of the unknown: where we were going and what our next assignment might be, for as green replacements we were merely pieces in a puzzle that would be put together later.

All any of us knew — and this was bad enough — is that we were going to a front line unit to replace someone who had been killed or wounded. I was not afraid but apprehensive, if that makes any sense. In the past I had always belonged to a specific unit whose daily routine and familiar faces provided a sense of security.

But being in limbo made me nervous, giving me the feeling you get when you move to a new town and leave all your friends behind. Now we were going to be surrounded by new friends and associates untested by the rigors of combat.

When apprehensive, time weighs heavily on your hands. In a bivouac, as we drew closer together, I visited with men I had gone through training and traveled with, wondering if I would ever see them again. We played cards and shared letters and memories of our civilian lives. Today, whenever I visit a war museum somewhere, I don't look for the guns or war machines, mostly I'm interested in more personal displays: homemade playing cards, diaries, pictures of loved ones, harmonicas, and small condensed Bibles, for example.

While I think many people might ignore these seemingly unimportant objects representing a simple soldier's life, anybody who has "been there" would properly recognize their valuable contribution to our well-being, which was so precious in the face of constant danger.

So far away from home, it is difficult to describe the lonely feelings of isolation, knowing that you are completely dependent on the Army to get you back again. Home seems completely unattainable, and you have no control but to survive until the war is over, while feeling that it may last forever.

I could only compare this feeling to when I was a young boy. My twin brother, sister and I set up housekeeping in a country school where my sister taught all eight grades in one room. The school was miles from the homes of many of the kids, and when they left school it was ghostly quiet, as only a country school yard can be. We had never experienced such an utter void in our lives, and it brought on a gut-wrenching feeling of homesickness. I suspect this was the reason my schoolmarm sister finally boarded with one of the neighbors some miles away, commuting to the school so my brother and I could stay home again.

When we finally left the quiet woods of our bivouac and moved toward our eventual destination, we moved through small towns and villages that had suffered less damage, probably because they were less important militarily, or perhaps because of the more rapid movement of troops as the Germans retreated eastward.

Still, we knew the people had suffered, for we saw them alongside the roads, women and children with baskets picking greens to eat, and we imagined their starvation diet after nearly five years of occupation and war.

As we drew nearer the front, we could hear the heavy guns firing, but the only G.I.s concerned were those who had been wounded and were returning to their units. To the rest of us, surprisingly, who had never heard enemy fire, it made little impression, for we had no experience with war's inconceivable madness.

Finally we arrived at our forward replacement depot, a group of partially destroyed buildings in a small farming community "somewhere in France." Here is where soldiers were funneled into the front lines, the combat veterans into their old outfits, and the new replacements, to await their assignments.

It was easy to tell them apart. The new men were boisterous and jovial, while the veterans were quiet and thoughtful, contemplating the risk they must face, some for the second or third time.

Eventually I would learn, as all of us would the hard way, that each time you returned to the front it becomes harder to face the horror and privation.

I would learn too that the men who eventually broke from nervous exhaustion and suffered shell shock were those returning from safety and forced back into this terrifying situation.

Life at the replacement depot, however, was not without its diversions. During this time I became acquainted with a French girl, Babette, an attractive and flirtatious jeune fille whose lover, an American sergeant, had to leave her behind when he returned to combat.

Abandoned and alone in area where other civilians had fled, Babette accepted me as her "protector," mostly because I could speak a little German which she had learned in school, but also, she told me, because I was not as clumsily aggressive as the other soldiers.

I felt that just because she was considered a "camp follower" there was no excuse for the others to be pawing and pressuring her. I treated Babette with respect and made no judgement on her morals, and she began seeking me out as her constant companion.

Still, I was young, healthy, facing death for the first time — and a long time away from any contact with the opposite sex. One day while we were out walking, Babette became quite amorous and cuddly and encouraged me to find a place away from the crowd.

Drifting through the blasted building of the replacement depot, we came upon a building that looked like some kind of storage shed. The roof had been blown away, there was a hole in the far wall I didn't notice, because of all the light from the building having no roof. There was what looked like a pile of damp bedding on the floor.

By this time were both getting very heated up, and Babette was cooperating nicely as I was trying to remove her skirt. I didn't notice, but she was facing the wall with the hole, while I faced the other way.

Suddenly, she began resisting my advances while talking very excitedly in French. Puzzled, I thought she might be objecting to the grim pile of bedding on the floor, but then she started shouting and pointing to the far end of the building.

There, through the hole in the wall, we could see a G.I. chow line that had strayed off-course to get a good view of our adventure.

Ironically, within an hour I was given orders to the front, while Babette disappeared, most likely attaching herself to another lonely G.I., though I kept her as a warm memory through the terrible months to come.

CHAPTER FIVE

At the Front

F rom the replacement depot I received orders to report as a radioman with the 1st Battalion of the 12th Infantry regiment, 4th Division, then holding the right flank of the Siegfried Line, which had recently been breached by General George Patton's Third Army.

Because I was a radioman, I ended up traveling as a lone private among a group of officers being assigned to their units. As we headed toward the front in the back of a small troop carrier, we soon were within range of the German's heavy artillery and the newcomers began getting nervous.

Traveling with us was a major who was to assign the officers their units and help them with their new assignments. There was also a young first lieutenant who, when the major told him he was to be a company platoon leader, became quite agitated and complained he was a Special Services officer and shouldn't be leading a combat team.

As we neared the front and the artillery fire increased, I took some pleasure in hearing the major tell him most emphatically that his "soft life and officer club days were over."

Aware of the high mortality rate of inexperienced platoon leaders in combat, the expression on the lieutenant's face was pure terror. The other officers looked away, embarrassed, and when he caught my eye I just shrugged and shook my head. Since I was a mere private, and, like him, new to combat, I could offer little sympathy. I'd only been in France a short time, but already I'd learned that war gave us little choice.

I arrived on the Siegfried Line, or "West Wall," the German's heavily fortified defensive position, to be met by Sgt. John Fondrk, who was a senior non-com with the radio section, and at the time was dug into an abandoned German pill box frying up a huge batch of "liberated" eggs for the section.

I immediately took a liking to the man, who wore thick glasses and a permanent frown that concealed his boyish exuberance, as well as an innate

CAPTURED GERMAN PILL BOX

sense of adventure that would get him, and me, into sometimes dangerous and awkward situations.

Fondrk, who was in charge of keeping our radios in good repair, a difficult task under combat conditions, was always devising ways to enhance our mutual comfort or safety. For example, he came up with the idea to add fifty feet of cord to our radio handsets, a relatively simple improvement that was a blessing to the radio operator. Instead of exposing ourselves to fire (radio operators were a preferred enemy target), we could remain in our foxholes or under cover and still maintain effective communication. We could have the handset (with all the controls on it), in the fox hole or the basement, and the radio on the outside of the hole. The 50 foot cord would even allow us to put the radio on the top floors of a building and operate it from the basement.

His adventurous spirit also made him a most interesting, and sometimes dangerous, companion. As a repair sergeant, he made it his unofficial task to replace batteries, deliver radio parts and make repairs on the front line, often during heavy combat when the radios were banged and battered (like their operators) from constant use.

There were supply platoons assigned to this job, but sometimes they were late in their deliveries and Fondrk took it upon himself to make sure his men were properly equipped. He cared for his men and, since we were attached to battalion command, recognized the vital importance of maintaining open lines of communication during combat.

Without effective communication, battalion commanders were unable to relay information to their troops, nor were they able to receive front-line status reports essential for command decisions.

Sometimes, when I was off duty, as a lark I would go with him to keep him company. For me the danger heightened the experience, especially when we ventured through enemy lines. Fondrk was a lousy navigator but he never seemed to worry about being in unknown territory.

We traveled in a jeep the sergeant had "acquired" for his personal use, and Fondrk's relaxed and often foolhardy disposition led us on blind wanderings between the lines where we were often challenged by our own troops or targeted by enemy mortar fire, which both of us carelessly disregarded. His standard comment would be, "well Nose —his nickname for me— I've done it again, this damned Jeep doesn't know enemy territory from friendly areas." That was the general height of his concern about a potentially dangerous condition, which we both soon forgot.

I was one of four radio operators assigned to battalion command, and since this is where combat missions were planned on the battalion level, with orders received from division or corps headquarters, the command post (CP) was always a beehive of activity. In addition to the battalion commander and his staff, there were other officers attached as liaison from the air corps, artillery, tank companies, rangers and other support groups. The communications officer represented the radio and wire section, and message runners and bodyguards completed the CP staff.

My battalion commander was Col. Charles T. Jackson, understandably a man under tremendous pressure but always a cool customer and well liked by his subordinates, including myself, who had great respect for the man.

Col. Jackson was also brave and unflinching under fire, sometimes to my dismay, as I accompanied him forward as his radio operator. If he failed to get good radio contact with his troops on the front-line, he would gather up his mobile CP personnel and haul ass forward, during which time we would draw enemy mortar and light artillery fire, and be in greater danger than the line companies.

The men up front were well dug in, and they also had the advantage of knowing the position of the enemy and his firepower. Us rear area guys, on the other hand, floundered about, at risk in areas we knew very little about.

Col. Jackson was also a man of great self-control, which made him a popular and successful commander. Once during a heavy mortar barrage, when I nearly destroyed my radio antenna ducking for cover, instead of shouting and chewing my butt out, which I deserved, he calmly reminded me that the radio was our only contact with our CP.

Breaking a slight grin, he said, "Really Harold, you must be more careful."

Whenever possible he treated his troops as equals, which is why our battalion had good morale and combat record.

Unfortunately, Jackson was eventually relieved and replaced by a less brave man. The new commander remained behind at his CP and sent his radio operators forward to establish relay stations. This meant going up to the front with a bodyguard and digging in during combat, a dangerous job, though I usually volunteered since it was a short stint that gave me a lot of time off.

There were four battalion radio operators, one for each post, and if all were manned there was no relief until one post was secured or shut down. Due to the exigencies of fighting the Germans, the Army gave little thought to our sleeping and eating, and much of the time we were stumbling around like zombies, gobbling field rations where we plopped down.

You might be on a radio for eighteen to twenty hours before you were relieved, especially at the main command post, and when you moved to another area, usually parallel to the front line, you might walk four or five miles along the main line of resistance. Some men got so they could actually sleep while walking, but usually we survived on catnaps, wrapping up in our coats and plopping down in the mud (it seemed to be raining all the time) and grabbing short minutes of sleep.

If the long march didn't poop you out, then certainly the lack of sleep did.

During quiet times, when were to be in position for a few days, the telephone platoon would run a wire out to us and we could shut down the radios until we went back on attack or enemy fire broke the phone lines.

Our radio messages were all voice transmissions, though we used predetermined groups of code letters for security, and these were usually changed week by week to counter any enemy interceptions.

Occasionally the Germans got playful, however, and we'd catch onto a German operator with a captured radio using our frequency. When we found them out, by using a prearranged message code, they would end their transmission with a string of curses — "Schweinhund! " and so forth, along with the usual threats of how they would soon destroy our "inferior troops."

By this time in the war, however, as we were penetrating Hitler's Third Reich, veteran officers and troops on both sides were becoming battle-weary from the war's unrelenting misery and occasionally displayed uncommon acts of compassion.

One day while I was on duty in the battalion CP a tired and rather bedraggled German officer approached with a white flag and, in English, asked politely if he might have some assistance.

We knew our troops had bottled up his unit for days, and he said conditions were horrible with many of his men wounded or dying. He requested stretchers and, if possible, some jeeps to help move his men, promising that everything would be returned.

For humanitarian reasons, and because of the German officer's quite painful honesty, the request was granted and our officers told him where the Germans should deliver the equipment when they were through — which, very carefully, they did some time later.

The generosity and compassion of our commander, and the humanity revealed by the German officer in pleading for his men, was very moving and provided me with an entirely new insight into the war: Except for few diehard fanatics, I sensed that troops on both sides felt the war had dragged on too long and should have been over.

Being a part of the battalion CP gave me valuable insights into what made our officers tick. The artillery liaison officer, in particular, was an amazingly hardworking guy who made a favorable impression on everyone around him.

The artillery liaison would sleep in the CP and was on call day or night. If we got a message from a line company telling us artillery was falling in their area, he could awake from a sound sleep and in seconds determine if it was ours or theirs. It was common for our artillery to change direction or lose "short rounds" that endangered our troops.

In a few more seconds he could relate coordinates to his gunners and direct our artillery to pound the enemy's guns, in most cases reducing or eliminating incoming fire.

If we were in a holding position and not actively engaged with the enemy, this artillery officer also liked to go "tank hunting," just as a farm boy might like to go squirrel hunting.

He would take a radio and find an observation position where he could direct fire onto a stray tank or two, and he had a very good success rate. The sport of it was he had to move quickly to keep the Germans from zeroing in on his radio, and the German gunners were real pros themselves.

Back at the CP he would recount the outing's success or failure —"I bagged three, two got away . . . " — much to everyone's amusement.

There were other officers, though, who earned the respect of no one and were considered merely bullshitters.

One of these, a young lieutenant with a Ranger platoon, came into the CP for a debriefing after a night patrol. His story was that he and his men had bravely destroyed a machine gun position with grenades, rifle fire and so forth, though I noticed the CO looking at him skeptically.

"So how many Germans were killed in the firefight?" the CO inquired.

"Well, I didn't go over and count them," the young Ranger officer said.

"So how did you know they were dead?" the CO persisted.

"Well, they quit firing."

The CO asked no more questions and asked for a written report instead, knowing the officer had lied, and soon we were rid of the Ranger platoon.

Ranger units were sometimes valuable in infiltrating enemy positions and obtaining information, and in fire fights with small enemy units, but they tended to be glory hounds at times, like the young lieutenant recounting his "mock patrol."

Needless to say, we "mocked" him, for most of us knew he had been hiding out within the perimeter during the hours he had allegedly been on patrol.

CHAPTER SIX

Huertgen Forest

O n Nov. 6, 1944, while in convoy with the 4th Division and headed to join the VII Corps, my outfit, the 12th Infantry Regiment, was tagged to support the 28th Division which had taken a hell of a beating trying to take the village of Schmidt, part of a battle that would be known as the "Bloody Huertgen."

Rerouted out of the convoy, the 12th, with its truckloads of cold, wet and miserably tired men, was driving deep into the forest, where we were dropped in a place as dark and gloomy as I've ever seen. It was like a cave with no lights, and you moved by instinct, blindly following the man in front of you. If he stopped suddenly, you slammed into him with your full field pack and rifle. Then the line would accordion in and out and you would hurry to keep up, stumbling over rocks, uneven ground and downed timber, making sure you didn't get lost in this spooky place that was like an old German fairy tale.

When we finally reached our position we were back under shell fire but so tired and disgusted that we plopped in the mud, curled up in our coats and tried to sleep.

Daylight added little to the gloom of the night before, since the canopy of fir trees was thick overhead, and we ate our K-rations cold since fires would have been visible in the dim light and we didn't want any additional harassment from the German artillery, which had the forest targeted with pinpoint accuracy.

The Huertgen Forest alone was a formidable natural enemy; add the tough

THE 12TH INFANTRY IN THE OPENING STAGES OF THE BATTLE OF THE HUERTGEN FOREST, NOVEMBER 1944.

German Army, now fighting desperately for its fatherland, and it was pure hell. The Germans were supposed to have been all but beaten by this time, and their stubbornness cost us some fine divisions that had fought valiantly since D-Day.

The overhead forest canopy was so thick that shells hitting the trees scattered the shrapnel over a larger area, and carried with it wood splinters in lethal concentrations, most of it coming straight down from above, so the forest itself added to the casualties and eliminated the small protection of getting behind a tree or some other barrier. Sound was also diffused and the blasts seemed magnified, so you were not sure which direction the fire was coming from.

Hitting the ground and lying flat merely exposed more of your body to danger, and you were probably better protected standing up, though natural instincts told you to hit the dirt.

Weary and frightened, under constant fire from the enemy, we began digging in, using our entrenching tools and helmets — or anything else that moved dirt — to get our bodies into the ground. Even if a hole was small, just big enough for your head, it provided some protection.

Under heavy fire, however, and between shell bursts, you dug more frantically. Soon a small hole became bigger, until, just as some forest animal, you were completely underground. Then, if you had enough strength left, you frantically cut limbs and scrabbled for small logs to cover your hole as added insurance against the shrapnel and splinters blasting overhead.

The Battle for the Huertgen Forest might be compared to the Battle of the Wilderness in the Civil War: Struggling blindly in the tangled undergrowth, against a formidable, well-armed and well-supported enemy entrenched in familiar terrain. Confusion and panic, and having no air and tank support, which American troops relied heavy upon, was traumatic and demeaning.

Unlike the Battle of the Wilderness, however, where it was hot, dry and men fought in the smoke and many were burned alive in the trees and undergrowth, the Huertgen was freezing cold, with rain and snow falling in one of the worst European winters in history, yet no less terrifying as we fought blindly in the dark and gloomy forest.

Infantry companies were decimated in the fierce fighting, and some were down to only a handful of veterans who had landed with their outfits on D-Day. This required that green, and starry-eyed replacements were thrown into the gaping ranks of units under fire. So stunned were these men that often they had to be led into holes already dug just to keep them alive. When they were wounded and brought into the aid station, many didn't even know what units they belonged to.

They learned quickly, however, and within days those who survived were transformed into dirty, glassy eyed, bewhiskered hulks of their former selves. And like the old-timers who themselves had never seen such fierce combat, moved and talked like zombies.

Since the Huertgen Forest battle was considered a side show to our major thrust into Germany, with its major objective the German city of Aachen, it didn't get the media attention it deserved. Another sad reality was that the campaign could have been avoided all together, since other plans were in place that would have accomplished the mission with far less casualties. But as we became involved, and it became increasingly impossible to extricate our troops, our units continued to be chewed up.

My insights and observations are mine alone, however, gleaned from contact with officers in battalion headquarters. But as a radio operator I had a seat on the "fifty yard line," so to speak, and was privy to information that, since I was sworn to secrecy, I was unable share with others in my company.

After the war, however, comparing notes with other veterans and from reading accounts of the battle years later, and from actual battle reports I obtained from the National Archives, I determined that the Huertgen Forest campaign was underrated. Many feel as I do, that the high echelon tried to minimize what was a command blunder and were intent on keeping it from the press and the Pentagon.

I think that those responsible for this heartbreaking, unequal match kept reporters out of the area intentionally, though a few, notably the author Ernest Hemingway, who was a combat correspondent (and some-

ERNEST HEMINGWAY (CENTER), DECEMBER, 1944

times illegal participant in the battle), were brave enough to enter this hell hole and provided accurate firsthand accounts of the debacle. In two months the casualties were about 25 percent, compared to about 10 percent in the previous fighting since D-Day.

The agony of this whole murderous campaign was heightened by the fact that what had started out as a routine acceleration of our quickly moving drive into Germany had bogged down into a succession of small, hard-fought battles that became particularly vicious, especially when probing the Siegfried Line, Hitler's allegedly impregnable "West Wall," which was honeycombed with steel-reinforced concrete bunkers and pillboxes.

Gloom and fog surrounded the pillboxes, their very presence was a foreboding evil. The few times I had the opportunity to examine a pillbox I had an overwhelming sense of dread. The interiors were cold and clammy, ventilated only by the firing slits or the door, if it could be left open. There were ventilation systems, but these were hand operated and it was hard to imagine anyone using them for any length of time, particularly during combat when they would be needed the most.

Even empty they conveyed a presence of the enemy: there were the smells of fear and dirty bodies, the debris of living in cramped quarters, and often, if a bunker had been used as an aid station, blood smeared over the walls and floors.

Buried deeply into the ground, the thick-walled pillboxes may have provided a false sense of safety, though these feelings must have been overridden by a claustrophobic sense of desperation and gloom; for these small fortresses were the last bastions against an invasion even the Germans knew would soon cost them the war.

Ironically, while the Germans were fighting a desperate last ditch battle for their homeland, their morale remained surprisingly high, while the morale of the American troops dropped sharply. Remember, we had come from a liberated area, France, Belgium and Luxembourg, where the people threw their arms around us, showered us with flowers, food and wine and welcomed us as liberators.

But now, suddenly, we were the hated invaders, even though we thought we were liberating the German people from a murderous regime. And by now they knew they had no chance of winning the war, despite Hitler's promise of saving the day with new and terrible "secret weapons," and their despair, with the pervasive gloominess of the tangled, nightmarish forest, created an oppressive environment for our troops.

Futility and frustration characterized the campaign. Every assault was hampered by our being a little too late with too few troops to control the situation, and there was always some unforeseen delay in taking our objectives, especially the crucial high ground where the Germans had the advantage in monitoring our movements.

Years later, having obtained a battle history of the 12th Regiment, I realize mistakes were made in committing entire divisions to operations that should have been carried out by much smaller units. By the time they discovered the enemy's strength and positions, it was too late to change plans, so they stumbled around taking enormous casualties.

Ineffectual attempts to extricate troops from these situations reflected poor leadership by combat officers who tended to downplay their predicament to higher command. This resulted in division or corps commanders holding back reserves, which were limited anyway, and ordering their hard-pressed field commanders to tackle impossible objectives.

As a result, some field officers were relieved of command, and it is quite possible that these failures in communication were compounded by subsequent reports that glossed over some dangerously crucial situations.

Naturally this comedy of errors provided an advantage to the Germans. Though their own supply problems were always critical, they were fighting on home ground and were extremely resourceful, and were capable of holding on tenaciously due to our inability to overwhelm them.

When we did have a small advantage, it was soon eliminated by our inability to get tank and artillery support, while the continual bad weather all but eliminated our air support.

On the narrow roads through this steep terrain it was easy to knock out tanks with mines and small artillery. Also, any deep shell crater could not be bypassed, and if they were filled in with dirt it was too soft to support our heavy armor. This necessitated the slow and sometimes nearly impossible tasks of the engineers, who were forced to widen roads by tearing into steep and rocky banks while under heavy fire.

All around us and well hidden in the woods, the Germans were dug into bunkers reinforced with thick logs. Having the advantage of familiar terrain, their mortars and light artillery were zeroed-in on predetermined coordinates and everything that moved down the forest trails was cut down. Main access roads tapered down to fire breaks and foot paths and it became a turkey shoot for the enemy.

Supply was hazardous, if not impossible, and our superiority in tanks and weapons was of no use in the steep canyons and along the narrow trails. It came down to moving supplies in jeeps, and finally to hand-carrying the ammunition and other supplies along roads and trails which soon became choked with bodies.

Quite often we had no choice but to walk across the bodies of our fallen comrades, which slowed our movements and made us vulnerable to withering fire, and one deadly route heaped with bodies became known as "Purple Heart Alley."

Because of the heavy woods and poor visibility, Germans and Americans sometimes just missed meeting each other along routes both were using, yet both sides were so battered and weary they probably didn't care.

A picture that still lives in my mind is that of a luckless soldier who had stepped on a mine. His upper torso was intact but from his lower body entrails and other body parts trailed for fifteen feet or more. It took many nights before I could sleep without imagining the poor man's agony.

The Graves Registration unit would attempt to remove the bodies as soon as possible because of the negative impact on morale, especially the new replacements, but could not always do so because of the heavy shelling that allowed no refuge from the onslaught.

More difficult was bringing up replacements and getting them into units where a few veterans remained alive and could to teach them how to survive. But if replacements and supplies were not available, or the fighting was too fierce, even the old combat veterans had a poor chance of survival.

Like the rest of us, the replacements had been well trained in infantry basics, but nothing can prepare a man for the horrors of combat. Many men prayed for strength not to succumb to cowardice, and even the most irreverent prayed in extreme circumstances. The saying, "There are no atheists in foxholes," became very apparent.

On the other hand, the Germans' stubborn delaying actions provided them with opportunities to reinforce their severely depleted ranks by rapidly moving troops from place, to place, allowing them to counterattack in force most effectively.

These counterattacks often culminated in vicious hand-to-hand struggles that were not really important to either side but whose inhuman brutality caused a terrible loss of life. Soon it became difficult to keep enough units together to hang replacements on.

While the early penetration of the Huertgen Forest seemed

GRAVES REGISTRATION UNIT, 12TH INFANTRY, REMOVES BODIES AS SOON AS POSSIBLE BECAUSE OF THE NEGATIVE IMPACT ON MORALE.

relatively easy, opposition stiffened as the battle continued, so it was like wading through quicksand and we eventually bogged down. And the more we bogged down, the Germans could funnel in troops and tanks from around Aachen, which we had yet to actively besiege.

As our tanks were destroyed, by panzerfausts (hand-held German rocket launchers) and small assault guns, their crews became demoralized and would poke their heads out of the turrets to shout, "Where is the infantry?" which they needed desperately to support them.

The unrelenting artillery fire stripped the trees of branches and blasted their tops, leaving the trunks shattered like giant toothpicks sticking up out of the ground. In the aftermath lay debris and dead bodies tossed together like garbage heaps, and the fury of the battle brought chills of apprehension.

The forest had been totally destroyed by shellfire — consider the furious and sustained fighting that could cause such destruction. Where a few well-placed rounds can cause enormous damage to a town, with its buildings clustered together, total destruction of a forest means hitting almost every individual tree.

Thinking back, it's now almost impossible to imagine the ferocity of the bombardment that had brought this immense forest to its knees.

Once as our battalion CP was on the reverse slope of a steep hill whose opposite slope faced the enemy, heavy artillery shells were passing over our heads continually. The hill was so steep that the rounds carried over us and we were entertained by the sounds they made: a distinctive whirring sound different from that of the deadly bits of shrapnel flying around.

Artillery and mortar shells are routine in an infantryman's existence and you ignore them as much as you can. Like everything else coming your way, they are the enemy trying to kill you; though long-range artillery is less personal, fired often from miles away, mortars are dropped upon you from a distance of yards, and are very personal indeed.

Machine gun and rifle fire is of course very unnerving, due to the close proximity of the enemy, but most casualties are sustained from artillery and mortar fire, whose relentless pounding breaks many soldiers from shell shock or combat fatigue.

Safe in our CP, we could imagine the hell endured by our front-line companies, where men were being shelled and machine-gunned with no possibility of getting out unless they were wounded. I often wondered what kind of training or condition would make a man stay there and take this kind of abuse. Was it patriotism, devotion to duty or just plain discipline that kept a man doing what he was told to do, even if it meant he might be killed or severely wounded?

Perhaps more realistically, it was the simple fact of not wanting to let his comrades down, which I would learn from bitter experience: hanging in there with only the slim, bitter hope of receiving a "million dollar wound" that was not life threatening but would get you out of this hell, if only for a while.

We were told in basic training that if we were wounded we would get prompt medical attention, be evacuated immediately and our troubles would be over, at least temporarily. If not, we had been frightened for nothing, and being killed had its own grim reward: we would be out of it forever, though these assurances provided little comfort when facing a determined enemy doing all he could to kill us.

Worse than being killed, however, and something that every soldier dreaded, was being wounded and left alone to suffer on the battlefield.

Try to imagine people being hurt or terribly maimed in an industrial or automobile accident, then multiply that tragedy by thousands. Now narrow your focus onto one individual and his anticipation of injury or death; not coming unexpectedly from some unanticipated source, but everywhere around you.

Now put yourself in the place of that soldier, knowing the odds are stacked against you. Some men knew at the time they were hit that their wound was fatal, so imagine the trauma of realizing you were going to die on some filthy, debris-strewn battlefield far from home and family, where no one seems to give a damn. The men in your unit feel your pain but are too busy keeping alive to show compassion. When you are dead, you are just a zero to the Army.

My first encounter with a dead comrade left an impression that remains indelible to this day. I was walking with a couple of buddies through an area that had been shelled heavily. As we climbed over some downed trees, I noticed the body of a soldier propped against a log as if someone had been trying to make him comfortable.

This poor soul had the top of his head blown off, and the remains of his skull looked like a shattered coconut shell. Not knowing why, I made the foolish mistake of stooping down to get a closer look, and even today I cannot understand my morbid curiosity.

My comrades, who were more battle hardened than I, had wisely gone on ahead and I ran quickly to catch up with them. I'm not sure they knew what I'd been doing, but no one mentioned my lagging behind and none of us said anything about it. It was a stupid thing to do, and for the next few days I was obsessed with the man's horrible death, as in my mind I can still see him lying there today.

In today's cynical times, when the battles of World War II seem as remote as Civil War battles to many Americans, we forget that every soldier in combat is doing a heroic deed in facing the enemy and suffering war's terrible day-to-day danger and deprivation, mostly out of a sense of patriotism to his country or loyalty to his comrades.

Civilians and, quite often, rear area support troops failed to understand or appreciate the front-line combat infantryman who was constantly in harm's way. Incredibly, I never heard an infantryman complain that he deserved special recognition. The well-deserved awards and medals they received represented only infinitesimal tokens of their gallantry.

As a private soldier and minor participant, I was too frightened and busy just keeping alive, and certainly in no position to question those with my fate in their hands. All I knew is that it was pure hell; a chaotic nightmare of shrieking shells and explosions, pierced by the cries of the wounded and dying, while others were left to consider the near and very real possibility of death.

If the hail of deadly and accurate enemy fire wasn't enough, there were other dangers from the random mishaps of war. One day, though we couldn't see it through the dense trees of the forest, there was a dogfight between German and American fighter planes directly overhead. During the aerial battle, an American pilot, unaware of our positions, jettisoned his spare fuel tanks onto a neighboring battalion, spreading flames through the helpless bastards screaming below.

After days of being constantly under fire and enduring a maelstrom of explosions and flying steel, I found myself eventually immune to the omnipresent danger and accepted combat as a simple condition of "kill or be killed," and let fate determine the outcome.

To me, at least, the rigors of combat were more tolerable than the harsh day-to-day existence of the infantryman, which during that bitter winter in the Huertgen Forest, with rain, snow and freezing temperatures, forced us to burrow like animals preoccupied with basic survival.

Sometimes our boots froze to the ground, our clothing and bedding were wet and filthy, we ate cold rations and constantly battled hypothermia, and often we were so numb from the cold that keeping warm took precedence over the dangers of enemy action. Forget about shaving or even washing, which we were unable to do for weeks at a time.

Adding insults to our permanent discomfort was the lack of rubber boots, which could have help prevent trench foot, and warm field jackets which more often found their way into the hands of rear area troops who wore them and swaggered around pretending they had been in combat

Still, we made the best of it by devising little improvements to our lifestyle. Sergeant Fondrk was very adept at this. He had been assigned a jeep to carry out his duties as a radio repairman, and that allowed him the mobility to practice his skills as a master scrounger.

Fondrk was like a lot of old soldiers who make themselves at home no matter where they are, and he was always scrounging something from regimental supply to feed us or make us more comfortable.

Often he would bring back "ten-in-one" rations, a boxed-up supply of canned and packaged food to feed ten men for one day. Unlike K or C-Rations, rather grim fare that fed one man for one day, ten-in-ones contained bacon, fruit and other goodies that, in a small group like ours, provided us with a feast.

Unable to build open fires that would draw enemy fire, Fondrk used the empty bacon cans to fashion a small stove and chimney that with a little bit of wood warmed his foxhole to a comfortable degree, allowing the radio section to drop in and warm themselves for short periods of time.

Fifteen minutes spent in Sgt. Fondrk's warm zone was a luxury that probably kept some of the boys from succumbing to frostbite and hypothermia.

Fondrk's centrally heated foxhole was still no match for some of the more elaborate dugouts created by our soldiers or inherited from the Germans as the battle went on. Foxholes became deeper and larger, transformed into bunkers that we covered with logs, lined with boards and disguised with fallen branches.

Two communications linemen I knew, who were assigned up front for five days at a time to repair severed power lines, spent most of their time improving and reinforcing their foxhole. When any of us came back from the front, having observed their frantic digging, we laughingly accused them of designing such an elaborate foxhole deep enough to include "two bends" to baffle incoming artillery fire.

Yet, no matter how hard we tried to improve our creature comforts, we were seldom warm or dry, continually filthy, hungry quite often and always afraid. It may sound ironic, but I'm sure a lot of men who seemingly sought danger in performing extreme acts of heroism were seeking distractions from their crude and uncomfortable way of life.

Whenever I met men from line companies, who were in constant contact with the enemy, I tried to imagine their home lives. These were fellows from all over the country, from the big cities and the small farming towns. There were a lot more farms in those days, and a lot of the farm boys, like myself, were in the Army.

I thought of individual members of my own family, knowing they couldn't begin to imagine the terrible environment of war: the pain, the suffering, the dying; how we felt or thought, our constant fear. They didn't know I was with a combat division, or where, since our mail was censored, and I couldn't relate to them the realities of my duties or the danger, yet knowing they would never understand.

Sometimes during battle I would let my mind wander back to South Dakota and the peaceful setting of farm life, milking cows and feeding animals. Driving a tractor or plowing or cultivating was a far cry from driving a jeep and ducking mortar shells. I could visualize my family going to church on Sunday and returning to a home-cooked meal, and I could almost taste the roast chicken, potatoes and gravy.

In combat, Sunday merely followed Saturday, and our home-cooked meal might be a can of beans, sometimes hot but more often cold, and sometimes, if you were unlucky, nothing at all.

Eventually, after two months of bitter fighting, the Battle of the Huertgen Forest began to wind down and most of us felt the war in Europe would soon be over. As the strains of combat eased, life seemed precious once more and the men became cautious, concerned they might get killed or wounded when the end seemed near. This was possibly what motivated the extreme caution of the two linemen we accused of constructing the foxhole with "two bends."

It had been a tough, frustrating, perhaps needless campaign that we had endured, fighting furiously and taking heavy losses, but which also had taken its toll on our enemy. The Germans had suffered as we had, but their resources of manpower and equipment were becoming irreplaceable.

Worse for them, they were forced back into their shattered homeland to lick their wounds and prepare for our final assault into Germany.

What we didn't know, and why the Germans had fought so stubbornly in the Huertgen Forest, was that the area would be a staging ground for a final, last gasp German counterattack ordered by the German Fuhrer Adolf Hitler: The Battle of the Bulge.

CHAPTER SEVEN

F Company

During the confused fighting in the Huertgen Forest the front seemed all around us. Though I was assigned to battalion headquarters, behind the main line of resistance (MLR) and in a position of relative safety, we were nevertheless under continual bombardment from German mortars and heavy artillery.

Since the heavy forest shadowed the effective range of our radios, we were sent forward occasionally to improve communications. Rather than being frightened, I began to welcome the experience. Despite my being at headquarters, I had great empathy for the troops slugging it out on the line, and felt it was my duty to share in at least a small part of the terrible business of fighting.

And by now, having endured an endless barrage, I had abandoned any concern for my personal safety and accepted the cruel fact that war was war and I was part of it. In our individual ways everyone shared death in the Huertgen. And like so many others, I eventually lost my fear of dying. If your number was up, that was it — I put my life in God's hands.

(However, whenever headquarters' personnel came forward with their radios there was an increase in enemy fire, and despite the urgent need for communications, our presence was often less than welcome.) One time there was an engineer company dug in at a hill flanking the enemy. They had been there for a week and had no activity from the enemy though they were close. But now that battalion headquarters was on the scene they were sure they were going to catch hell due to our many radio calls. They were not really hostile but I could sense the feeling that they were glad we were moving on.

When I went forward on my first day in combat, however naive and still untested, it almost became my last, and was the closest I ever came to being killed or wounded.

Because of poor radio signals, Colonel Jackson, our battalion commander was concerned about maintaining good communications with our line companies as they advanced. Gathering up his mobile command post, which included myself and another radio operator (in case one of us was killed, we noted ominously) we followed B and C companies into the front lines under a withering storm of German mortar and artillery fire.

Stupidly unafraid, I walked blithely along, packing my heavy radio and wondering why everyone else was so tense, all of them moving slow and low to the ground. I learned why in an instant, when a mortar round dropped nearby and the concussion picked me off my feet, knocked the wind out of me and tossed me into a shell hole where I lay like a rag doll.

That I survived at all was either beginner's luck or a miracle, and ironically, it was the forest itself that saved me. The heavy undergrowth muffled the blast and took the brunt of the shrapnel, leaving me unharmed but stunned and shaken, and certainly much wiser.

It was a lesson I remembered well. After that I hunkered down and crept along as tensely as the rest; perhaps even more so, for my buddies soon started kidding me about developing a "radar ear:" One ear growing larger and more sensitive to the sound of incoming shellfire.

Several days later we were sent forward again, having received word that 2nd Battalion had gotten itself into trouble and was nearly surrounded. Unable to reach the 2nd Battalion CP by radio, the colonel assembled a small group of us into a mobile command unit to move forward and establish contact.

Along with the colonel and his two bodyguards, the unit included the communications officer, a message runner (in case our radios were knocked out), and again, myself and another radio operator, so we knew there would be considerable danger.

Heading out under heavy artillery and mortar fire, we moved forward until we reached Company E, which was in reserve and had managed to establish contact with 2nd Battalion and other units fighting in the area.

Upon arrival, the colonel and his officers were invited to share a bunker with the E Company commander. Nearby was another bunker where I could see two wide-eyed infantrymen poking their heads out cautiously. They seemed to be in a subdued state of shock, and looking around I could see why. Lying around their hole in no particular pattern were three dead Germans who had obviously just been killed, for their bodies were still bleeding.

I figured the guys in the bunker were too shook up to ask them what happened. But seeing I was a newcomer, a GI in a hole farther down waved me over and told me the story: the Germans had surrounded the bunker and demanded the Americans surrender. With only a split second to act, the terrified GI's answered by tossing out hand grenades (which fortunately weren't tossed back), ending a kill-or-be-killed, "Mexican standoff." From the looks on the guys' faces you could tell just how close it had been.

By now we were drawing even heavier enemy fire, and since there was no room for myself and the other operator in the command bunker, the colonel relieved us of duty temporarily and told us to get our butts under cover.

Seeing our plight, a medic motioned us over and offered us shelter in his forward aid station. He had a hole large enough for himself and a wounded man, but since he was moving forward he told us we could move in, though first we had to help him move his patient, a poor bastard whose legs had been riddled by machine gun fire. We winced, feeling his pain, but the wounded guy managed a weak grin and told us not to worry since he was full of morphine and didn't feel a thing. Though his wounds would soon bring him terrible pain, we envied him in a way since he would soon be evacuated to safety.

After recovering our radios, we burrowed into the bunker and soon made contact with the temporary command post. To save batteries we were told to rely on the runner to convey messages, and I didn't envy that poor bastard moving around in the open under deadly enemy fire.

We were being pounded relentlessly, and the ground shook from the explosions while the air was filled with the whir and buzz of flying shrapnel. This continued throughout the afternoon and we were grateful for the shelter, which seemed safe enough for the time being.

Things grew worse, however, as the day wore on. Without our knowing it, the colonel and his staff pulled back, claiming they could not locate our position, and the runner disappeared and was never heard from again. We never knew if he had been captured or simply wandered off and was killed in the confusion. Worse, while our radios buzzed and seemed alive, we were unable to send

ENEMY FOXHOLES

or receive messages.

By dark the shelling had escalated, and mortar rounds were falling all around us. Soon they were falling directly onto our hole, though luckily fallen branches had piled up to reinforce the logs built overhead. It was also bitterly cold, and we could tell it was snowing because the shellfire filtered flakes down into the bunker.

It was during that long night, with the ground shaking and the German shells screaming out of the darkness, that I learned the truth of the adage: "There are no atheists in foxholes." Though I was certainly no "Bible thumper," I knew how to pray with a faith acquired in my God-fearing farming community. And my foxhole buddy, who told me he had never gone to church nor believed in God, and by his own admission had led an immoral life, in desperation and with a feeling of complete helplessness against the incessant shelling, prayed sincerely alongside of me.

There is no way to describe the feelings of helplessness and abandonment one endures while being pinned down under heavy fire. It was impossible to move anywhere outside the bunker, and I could not fault the colonel and his staff for leaving this chaos when they could; nor did we blame them for not venturing out to find us since we knew that would be suicide.

At times like those, when reality has been shattered into moments of pure terror, it was every man for himself and only God could determine the outcome.

By the next morning, the barrage had eased into sporadic mortar fire that came down after the Germans zeroed in on the cigarette smoke trailing up out of our bunker. When only one man smoked, we were not shelled, but when both of us smoked at the same time, the smoke was concentrated enough that they could see it. We were so inexperienced that it took several dangerous hours for us to figure this out. This is how we were able to figure out that it was daylight as the enemy could see our concentrated cigarette smoke in the daylight.

When the mortars finally died down, we began to dig out and found our bunker covered with several feet of fallen branches. These had provided added protection but had kept us in the dark, and we had to remove half of the Huertgen Forest to claw our way outside.

In the daylight we saw that our radio had been hit and was full of shrapnel, though the batteries were still undamaged, explaining the problem of the night before. Moving around cautiously, we saw no one else around and the CP bunker had been abandoned.

Scrounging through the empty bunkers we eventually found a radio that was still intact, but the battery case had been destroyed. We assembled our good battery case on the still intact radio and managed to reach our CP, where they were surprised to learn we were unhurt and still alive. We also told them things had also quieted down, and when they learned we had patched together a radio we "volunteered" to deliver the unit to F Company, which was surrounded and needed communications to coordinate a breakout with other units in the area.

No rest for the wicked, I thought. But we were glad to have survived the night, and it was a quiet and beautiful morning, dazzlingly bright beneath a layer of new snow that made the world seem real again. Headquarters could only give us rough directions, but with the bright sun to warm and guide us, we set off cheerfully to find F Company.

It seemed to us that the Germans had pulled out, and since there was no shellfire we were filled with confidence. For hours I wandered blissfully with my radio buddy, as if on a pleasant adventure, enjoying a day all the more beautiful after the terrible night before.

Or maybe we were just stupid, daring the Germans to spoil our little outing. Whatever the reason I was not afraid, nor was my buddy, even though we had to pass through German lines.

We never discussed this situation, even later; as I never heard soldiers in the field discuss fear, sensing perhaps that fear unspoken might never exist or would disappear. Neither of us had been this close to the front, and not knowing what to expect we foolishly ignored the seriousness of our situation.

Also, I suppose we figured that since there were only two of us the Germans wouldn't consider us a threat, while a regular front line soldier would have been more cautious. But we just plodded along dumbly through the snow, warmed by the bright sunshine and glad to be alive, until by luck or accident we eventually stumbled upon F Company.

Our arrival at F Company, however, brought us back to war's grim realities. The company had been hit hard, there were many dead and wounded, and those who were wounded but could still walk were struggling to care for the seriously injured. I was particularly moved by one man, who had been shot through the face, attempting to care for a man whose body had been torn apart, and all around us we saw the bandages of more obvious wounds. I shuddered in the bright warm sunshine, chilled suddenly by the carnage around us.

My heart sank seeing these poor surrounded troops who had fought so desperately, unable to get their dead or wounded out or to get badly needed supplies into their besieged position.

As we stood there numbly, I saw a lieutenant waving frantically and urging us in harsh whispers to get down and keep quiet since there were Germans all around us; a fact we two stumblebums had ignored, still wandering about carelessly like two Sunday hikers back in the States.

As we approached, the officer grimaced and asked us if we would take a look at his back and see if he had taken a round. I could see a hole in his cartridge belt, and tracing it through thick layers of his clothing I discovered a spent bullet that had barely penetrated his skin, though he had felt nothing during the heat of battle.

The company commander was grateful for the radio, which would allow him to reach his battalion commander, but there was little else we could do for these men trapped in hell. We had no idea if they had food or adequate ammunition, but we had no food and hadn't eaten ourselves since the day before.

The wounded seemed to be getting adequate field care from the hard-pressed medics, however, and most of the men I could see, were walking wounded, still capable of firing their weapons. Others, however, were desperately in need of intensive care at a battalion aid station or hospital.

One of these was a poor bastard who had been cut down by a machine gun, and we told the C.O. we would try to carry his litter back to our battalion CP, which was through enemy lines.

This would mean packing a stretcher along a narrow access road known as "Bloody Alley." We had come to the front through this firebreak and knew it was under fierce and constant shelling by the Germans.

MEN WHO FOUGHT HARD DURING THE BATTLE OF HUERTGEN FOREST WERE REWARDED.

Grabbing up the stretcher, we took off, trusting to luck and prayer, but with little confidence that we wouldn't be wounded or captured. Miraculously, we made it through with little difficulty, perhaps because two men and a litter were little threat to the Germans, who often showed compassion to our wounded.

Not that the trip was

uneventful, for the terrain was rough and hard to travel. When the shelling became severe we had to find cover, tossing ourselves and the injured man into any hole we could find. The wounded man, who was in terrible pain, bravely told us to forget about him and care for ourselves. But whether he cared, or even thought about it, he must have known he had little chance without us, so he wanted to be sure that were safe.

We didn't discuss it, but all of us were aware that, with luck, his chances of survival were much better than ours. His "million dollar wound" would get him out of this hell hole where we would be stuck for a long time.

Later, for our success in delivering the radio to F Company, and for carrying out the wounded man, we were written up for the Bronze Star. When I learned of this, I asked that it be canceled. We had more or less been bumbling around when we reached F Company, and I felt we hadn't done anything heroic enough to deserve it. Our battalion communications officer insisted we both should accept the award, however, arguing that the paperwork had already been sent in and reminding us that the Bronze Star was worth five points toward early discharge. I sensed, however, that underneath he was feeling guilty about abandoning us on the front line.

During the awards' ceremony I felt conspicuous as hell lined up with soldiers who had fought long and hard under sustained fire. Eventually, though, I managed to rationalize that what the military defines as "above and beyond the call of duty" for one class of service might be routine for another.

As for F Company, I learned later that, along with two other companies, it had been surrounded for five days and had suffered terrible losses and casualties. I still envision those poor wounded soldiers dragging themselves into battle, enduring terrible pain and fear while fighting desperately with little hope of survival.

AG 201 - Knittel, Harold W. (Enl)

Subject: Unexpurgated Citation to Award of Bronze Star Medal.

To: Private First Class Harold W. Knittel, 37074228,
Headquarters Company, 1st Battalion, 12th Infantry.

Citation:

"HAROLD W. KNITTEL, 37074228, Private First Class, Headquarters 1st Battalion, 12th Infantry, for heroic service in connection with military operations against an enemy of the United States in the vicinity of Hurtgen, Germany, on 11 November 1944. Private KNITTEL carried a radio to a rifle company fighting in almost inaccessible terain while the only available route was constantly bombarded by mortar, artillery and rocket fire. In spite of the extreme danger, he bore the radio through deep muddy roads, steep inclines, dense underbrush, and mined forests for more than a mile. Private KNITTEL successfully reached the front and established radio contact although he narrowly escaped injury from flying shell fragments. Because of poor weather conditions, he was forced to expose himself constantly to insure adequate reception. On the following day when his relief arrived, he again delivered a radio to another company through heavy artillery fire. This equipment was indispensable in enabling the company commanders to communicate with the battalion command post during an important operation. Private KNITTEL's courage and devotion to duty reflect credit upon himself and the military service."

BY COMMAND OF MAJOR GENERAL BLAKELEY:

FRANK C. CASTAGNETO,
Lieutenant Colonel - A.G.D.,
Adjutant General.

CHAPTER EIGHT

Reflections

B attered by the fighting in the Huertgen Forest and badly in need of rest and recovery, we were sent into Alsace-Lorraine, a region of Northeastern France on the German border that had passed back and forth between the two countries since the Franco-Prussian War.

The people spoke German but considered themselves French, or considered themselves German but spoke French; I was never quite sure since it depended upon who you talked to. Whatever, the region had been under Prussian control after 1871, became French again after World War I, and had been under Nazi control since 1940.

This time around, however, the allies considered the Alsatians to be French rather than German nationals, and therefore a liberated people, so we were allowed to fraternize. Having some knowledge of German, which I had learned from my grandmother back in South Dakota, but spoke quite poorly, I quickly made friends with the Alsatians and took a stab at sorting out their confusing heritage.

This confusion was personified in a confrontation I encountered in a small town where we were bivouacked for a few days, and where a little old woman was being shunned and vilified by the town's residents amid rumors she and her late husband had collaborated with the Nazis.

It made for great gossip among the townsfolk, who ranted and raved about the woman, but I began to get suspicious when there seemed to be damn little proof of all the "terrible things" the old couple had allegedly done.

I began to wonder if perhaps the other villagers weren't protesting too much, throwing off flak to cover their own shaky relationships with their recently departed occupiers.

Finally, I asked the old woman about what had gone on. All she would say was that she was aware of the town's animosity but didn't really give a damn, adding vehemently that it was nobody's business what she and her husband had done, and that included "snoopy Americans."

Crinkling up her wise old face, she would only admit that she and her husband had lived there all their lives, through two wars, and had managed to survive under the "old Germans," the French, and the "'new Germans' sent by Hitler."

Then she said cynically, "It's all the same to me. War is war and nothing but stupid foolishness between men. I am old, I live and let live and let others do as they want. I've lived under the Germans, the French . . . Now we will live under the Americans. So what?" She shrugged. "The main thing is to stay alive."

After our conversation, the other townspeople kept their distance and were no longer friendly despite my best efforts. From what I gathered, they were afraid that the little old lady had spilled the beans on them all, which was probably true.

History would eventually reveal and revile considerable collaboration between the Nazis and some segments of the French population during the German occupation of France.

But in Alsace-Lorraine, a hybrid region where French and German armies had tromped back and forth for generations, interpretations of loyalty and collaboration were muddled and it was difficult to point accusing fingers at anyone.

While we relaxed in this small town, someone had discovered a barber shop open and word quickly spread among the GI's, who, after months of fighting in the forest, resembled filthy, hairy trolls. The going price for a shampoo and haircut was about forty cents' American, and I thought at the time that a greedier barber might have gotten rich off of all the dirty GI's who crowded into the tiny shop.

I knew from experience, however, that things would change very soon. When it was my turn in the chair, I remembered when we first arrived in France and prices were still cheap. A good bottle of wine sold for about fifteen cents, an apple pie was about a quarter, and despite the demand, prices stayed down because the troops were mostly low-paid infantry — but liberators nevertheless.

Prices shot up quickly, however, when things settled down and after an Air Corps unit moved in and began throwing big money around. Wine went to three dollars a bottle, apple pies were suddenly two dollars apiece, while the lowly infantry gathered up its C Rations and left their fleeting paradise to find or fight for another.

Paradise for the weary, dirty, ground pounding infantryman was when and where you found it, and could be described as anyplace warm, dry,

· 48 ·

clean or away from combat, though "paradise" in wartime could be dangerously deceptive.

And if the Germans didn't kill or wound you, as we found out one night, there were other little critters fond of American blood.

One night we stumbled into a remote farming village and made our bivouac in a small barn that any old farm boy, after one whiff of the place, could tell had been used for goats.

Despite its gamey smell, the barn was clean and dry and we quickly made ourselves at home, unrolling our blankets over thick beds of straw that allowed us the first good night's sleep we'd had in days.

Trouble came the next morning with an itching and burning in our crotches and other hairy areas that brought us out of our beds to dance like madmen in the warm sunshine, cursing and, as someone suggested, wondering if "Uncle Adolf" had unleashed a new secret weapon upon us.

Our enemy was some very ambitious and hungry goat lice (we accused them of being German), who as the sun warmed our clothes became quite active and aggravating.

As the day wore on, however, they began to shun us. We were puzzled for a while, but eventually figured that they must have preferred goats' blood to ours. This was no surprise, since by now we probably smelled worse than most of the goats in France or Germany.

Soon after losing our little friends from the goat barn, we were standing outside contemplating our good fortune when sounds of horns honking caught our attention. Coming up the road was a motorized unit of the French First Army, their vehicles filled with laughing and shouting girls crammed in among the soldiers.

We weren't sure where they were coming from or going (they were headed east), or when they had last engaged the enemy. But evidently it had not been too recently because they were clean, fresh and quite merry; perhaps because of the young women, who were pretty and flirtatious, and who at that moment could have done more for our morale, certainly, than a swarm of goat fleas.

The French column passed by us a ways, then stopped abruptly before a farmhouse and began harassing an old German man (perhaps the goat farmer? I thought) who looked back at them with an expression of weary resignation.

After being roughed up by the French soldiers, who demanded they give him some wine, the old man shuffled slowly into his half-ruined house and returned a short time later with an armful of bottles he handed over to the French. One of the soldiers, an arrogant young man, tasted a few bottles then, apparently displeased with the quality, spit the wine back in the old man's face and started slapping him around.

Ordered back inside, the defeated down old man made the trip again, returning with a vintage that apparently pleased the French, who pushed him away rudely and caused him to stumble. I felt sorry for the old guy. He was our enemy, or at least a German, and even now, when we knew teenage boys and old men were being thrown into the gaping ranks of the German Army, I felt he was long past doing anyone any harm.

Yet I could also understand the attitude of the French, who had endured more than four years of German occupation, and had been invaded by their old enemy three times in the last century.

The wine was good though, the French having left us a few bottles before they moved down the road. As we became more experienced wine scavengers I learned, as the French knew, that civilians left their poorer wine out for easy picking, while hiding or burying the good stuff.

Catching on, I used my limited knowledge of German to establish working friendships that soon allowed me to barter American cigarettes, chocolate and soap for some better vintages hidden behind walls or cellars or buried in fields out behind the barn.

By this time we welcomed any small diversions from the horrors of frontline combat. But even after the terribly brutal fighting we endured in the Huertgen Forest, these minor diversions did little to lift our spirits or alleviate the difficulties of life in the field. Though the war in Europe would be over in less than six months, no one had told us or the Germans, and as far as we knew it could go on forever. Under these conditions it was impossible to conceive of the war ending, let alone dream of returning home to the States.

The winter of 1944 was one of the worst winters in European history and we were living out of doors with very little shelter. It took great effort to just stay warm and dry, to keep from getting frost bite, trench foot or hypothermia — and if we did dream, there was no room in our dreams for luxuries. All we wished for was warmth, a bath, clean dry clothes, decent food, and a good long sleep in a soft bed away from the sound of shellfire.

Because my duties required me to visit the front intermittently, I was able to observe the men who fought and died there, and I tried very hard to bring back accounts that were accurate and objective.

The personal observations of men fighting in the front lines impart more feeling and reality to events than dispassionate historians are able to convey. Letters home are much more interesting than mere accounts of battles or troop movements and impart a special flavor of truthfulness to the everyday anxieties and torments of the combat soldier.

It would be difficult to accurately portray this horrible, upside down world unless you'd been there, and those who had experienced the unique terror of combat were reluctant to talk about it, perhaps thinking that if they kept quiet it would be more quickly forgotten.

One of the most terrifying experiences anyone can endure is being caught in a sustained artillery or mortar barrage, which I was two or three times, without any hope of escape. You become paralyzed by feelings of overwhelming helplessness and vulnerability and can do nothing more than lie there and take it. You are certain that each shell has your name on it, and the next one will rip into your foxhole and tear you to pieces.

The noise is deafening, a howling, screeching cacophony of inhuman sound that surrounds you and is punctuated by violent explosions and whirlwinds of concussion that toss your body around like a rag doll. In the aftermath your muscles are stiff and sore, as if you've been in a fight and whacked all over by a heavy club, but the soreness is from tensing your muscles in sheer terror.

Helpless and trapped under heavy and sustained artillery barrage, some men have been known to go mad, literally tearing the hair out of their heads or even killing themselves, while many others succumb to "shell shock."

The only comparable experience was when I was a boy of ten and my brother and I got caught in a vicious hail storm. We ducked under a shed with a tin roof, and the sound was like cannon balls coming down. We thought the storm would never end, and that the wind and hail would in some way kill us, and we were terrified.

Yet imagine that long ago South Dakota hail storm magnified a thousand times and you get some idea of what it's like to live through an artillery barrage.

Most soldiers I knew, however, would rather discuss their poor living conditions than their harrowing experiences of being shot and shelled. Enemy fire is something you had little control over, but loud griping about your day-to-day miseries, even if it did no good, at least let you blow off steam and in some small way made you feel like you had some control over your anger and frustration.

Perhaps because I was a country boy, I rather enjoyed living outdoors, at least when the weather was nice and we weren't under enemy fire. And being a romantic, it was sort of an extension of the life I had dreamed about, and sometimes actually lived, as a youth back in South Dakota.

Back then, we lived in a house on the Rosebud Reservation and most of my boyhood playmates were Sioux Indians. During the day we ran together like early Plains Indians, catching fish from a nearby stream and cooking them outside over an open fire. We learned how to hunt small animals and find edible roots and berries. Sharing these experiences offered a freedom and rare innocence that had all but disappeared as we grew to adulthood.

In the evenings the white boys would return to their families and civilization. Most of the Indian boys, however, lived in tents, and in the evenings the little valley cut by the stream filled with aromatic smoke from their campfires. Their families lived, for the most part, outside and did their cooking and household chores outside, just as we did in the mud of France and Germany, and I wondered if any of those Indian boys were fighting somewhere in Europe and remembering those same blissful summers from long ago.

The outcome of great battles often depends on the lowly action of a single rifleman in an infantry company; the "private soldier" who only months before was a civilian selling shoes, milking cows or just getting out of high school. Inevitably, however, the harsh crucible of combat tempers this soft civilian into a veteran whose only task is to stay alive and, as one battalion commander put it bluntly, "kill the sons-of-bitches!" Meaning of course the Germans, who for the most part were skilled veterans and very tough to kill, and who were led by career officers who fought us brilliantly and tenaciously even as they knew the war was lost.

Our own officers, quite often, were hardly different from the men who served under them. Many were civilians: ROTC graduates, officer training school graduates ("90-Day Wonders"), others were promoted from the ranks of senior NCO's, or commissioned for outstanding service or heroism.

Front line company officers carried a very heavy burden. While a lone infantryman had only himself or his buddy to think about, a company officer had to care for his men while motivating them to attack, often against formidable odds and with the least danger, and try to keep himself alive as well.

In addition, he had to provide for food, medical attention and ammunition, all the while keeping his junior officers safe and effective.

With all these responsibilities, there was the need to communicate with battalion headquarters to coordinate attacks, which often had to be done in person since the enemy would tap into our wire or monitor captured radios.

This was usually done at night after we were dug in, so it was particularly hazardous since they were sometimes shot at by their own men, especially the new replacements, who were jumpy as hell.

Another risky task was going to the aid of the wounded. It should be noted that where I was, at least, men would brave mine fields and enemy fire to retrieve even a single casualty, sometimes carrying a wounded comrade for a considerable distance to an aid station.

The medics, whose duty it was to treat or move casualties under heavy fire without regard to their own safety, were some of the bravest men I ever saw, though they carried no weapons and many were conscientious objectors.

At times we took care of the enemy wounded, and this basic humanity was occasionally shared, particularly after fierce and exhaustive battles when both sides were overwhelmed by the suffering around them.

Though we had seen such suffering in the terrible fighting in the Huertgen Forest, we were to experience it again very soon in the last-gasp German offensive known as The Battle of the Bulge.

CHAPTER NINE

Battle of the Bulge

E arly in December 1944, our corps commander decided to give our division a much needed rest, which allowed us to regroup, replace lost equipment and fill ranks depleted during the bloody month-long campaign in the Huertgen Forest.

I remember how peaceful it was, and how contented we felt as we pulled out of the range of the German mortars and artillery, many of the men singing Christmas carols and enjoying the relief of being away from the rigors of heavy combat.

Since we belonged to battalion headquarters and had been spared much of the heaviest fighting, our good spirits were not often shared, however, by many officers and men from the line companies who had lost so many of their comrades.

I always felt a little sad and guilty that we in battalion headquarters were able to move in and out of the high danger areas, while the line companies had no choice but to dig in and take it.

Yet everyone seemed in better spirits when we arrived at a small German village where we were allowed to bivouac in homes that were more or less intact and offered us much-needed relief from living like rats underground.

Even those of us in battalion command felt we deserved this respite as a Christmas present after surviving the Huertgen Forest campaign. And though the German villagers were understandably hostile when we arrived, they warmed quickly after Sergeant Fondrk, my resourceful old buddy who could fix anything, surprised them with a

THE GERMAN VILLAGE, VILLEDIEU LES POELLES, WERE THE 12TH DIVISION SPENT CHRISTMAS.

Christmas gift from the conquering "Amis."

While wandering around the village the next day Fondrk and I discovered a small electrical substation that had been knocked out in the fighting. The building was still in really good shape, and after prowling around Fondrk found that the feeder lines were still intact and all that was required to get the station up and running was to fabricate a fuse, which he soon did, lighting up the town to the surprise and gratitude of the residents who had been anticipating a dark and gloomy Christmas.

It worked out for us as well. Now we had lights to read by and, more important, a radio to listen to, though about the only thing we could understand on the French and German stations was the music. After weeks of living like animals in the cold and mud of the forest, this was "hog heaven," as our Southern boys would say.

Though the village had been secured and occupied, German troops remained dug in across a small river that was less than half a mile away, and so close that we could hear the rumble of large motorized vehicles, probably tanks, maneuvering around their positions.

With the Germans close by, some of our men became dangerously curious. One day while on perimeter guard my buddies and I spotted two soldiers prowling around near the river, which was some distance away. Unable to tell whether or not they were Germans, we cranked off a couple of rounds over their heads to stir up some reaction.

Almost immediately we saw a small white flag, and as the men approached with their hands in the air we identified the culprits as a red-faced lieutenant and sergeant from our outfit. They hadn't told any-one where they were going, and were lucky the lieutenant was carrying a white handkerchief instead of the standard-issue olive drab.

It soon became a joke in our unit to never go anywhere without your "surrender flag," though after this incident everyone stayed pretty much close to our lines.

Hard to comprehend by those who have never been in combat is that both sides at times observed unofficial "working hours." When it was quiet and we were not under orders to attack, we more or less ignored the presence of the enemy, who evidently did the same for us.

Between attacks both sides would "close up shop," so to speak, and even at times when were behind or very close to German lines, if it was "after hours" we might be ignored.

One time, during the Battle of the Bulge, Fondrk and I were in a jeep delivering radio batteries to the front lines. It was snowing heavily, visibility was poor and we were wandering aimlessly from unit to unit without paying too much attention to where we were.

Suddenly, we were challenged rudely at a road block, covered by a couple of nervous American G.I.s armed with a rifle and a machine pistol. After identifying ourselves, we were told they were jittery because we had just passed through a town occupied by the Germans. Then they said to listen carefully, and through the heavy silence of the falling snow we could hear the Germans shouting loudly and singing Christmas songs.

We supposed they had found someone's wine cache, as they sounded quite drunk, and they certainly hadn't challenged us as we blundered through their area. Perhaps they were too drunk to care, we thought nervously, or maybe they were just observing an "unofficial truce" when we sped through town.

Another time, the day before the huge German counterattack that would become the Battle of the Bulge, we were on a company sized patrol in the vicinity of Bastogne, Belgium, moving along in a column that was strung out for some distance along the road.

I was the radio operator at the front of the column, and though we had been wandering around in circles for hours, we saw no evidence of enemy activity. The next day, however, when all hell broke loose, we learned the Germans had been all around us but did not want to tip us off to their attack.

This was the Germans' Ardennes Offensive, better known to history as the "Battle of the Bulge" — a last-gasp attempt by the Third Reich to stall and possibly divide the Allied forces.

Planned by Hitler personally, and under the command of Field Marshal Gerd von Rundstedt, the Germans had somehow managed to amass the 5th and 6th panzer armies, as well as the 7th Army, a force which totaled 70 divisions in all, 15 of them armored, though many were under strength and needed rest and new equipment.

Allied intelligence had been keeping an eye on this powerful German force, which it knew was being held in reserve east of Aachen, but lost track of it early in December, largely because poor weather hindered air surveillance.

Anticipating continued bad weather, the Germans had planned their invasion to coincide with a massive winter storm that was predicted to linger over the front, grounding allied planes that in good weather controlled the skies.

Against the German force stood only the American VIII Corps, four divisions stretched over some 75 miles, between Aachen in the north and Alsace-Lorraine to the south.

The attack began December 16, and was a complete surprise, forcing back and even routing American forces in some areas. One area which refused the German offer to surrender was in Bastogne. "Nuts!" was the alleged reply of General MacAuliff, the American commander of the 101st Airborne Division. They were surrounded, yet fought with dogged determination — with cooks and clerks, bakers and bandsmen, the walking wounded and anyone else who could hold a rifle, fighting on the line.

The objective of the German offensive was to break through the Ardennes and cross the Meuse River, then swing north and northwest to divide British and American forces and eventually take the Belgian port of Antwerp. If successful, the offensive might have delayed or even changed the outcome of the war.

However, by December 26, after penetrating allied lines by 60 miles and in some places only four miles from the Meuse, the Germans ran out of gas — both literally and figuratively. Skies had cleared by December 23, bringing swarms of fighters and bombers, while allied forces mustered reserves and counterattacked: British and American divisions from the north under command of British Field Marshal Montgomery, and the American Third Army from the south under Gen. George Patton.

It was the Germans last offensive of the war. They made a last savage attack on Bastogne which held, and a surprise low-level air attack on allied forward airfields on Jan. 1, 1945 — yet by Jan. 16, it was all over. The Germans retreated behind their border after irreplaceable losses of equipment and 120,000 killed or wounded.

Following the battle, Field Marshal Montgomery, who was often at odds with American commanders, commented graciously, "The Battle of the Ardennes was won primarily by the staunch fighting qualities of the American soldier."

American troops had done almost all the fighting, and they had also suffered almost all the losses.

When the Germans launched their offensive, my regiment, the 12th, took the main thrust of units of the 7th Panzer Army, which were attacking from the northeast down toward one of their main objectives, the City of Luxembourg.

The fighting was fierce, desperate and often heroic. One American platoon was holed up in a three-story building and put up a hell of a fight while the building was destroyed around them. They started on the roof, but ended up fighting in the basement. When things cooled down, they counted more than a hundred dead Germans outside the building, part of a full company of German mechanized infantry that had attacked their position.

During the intense fighting our ranks were decimated. Having no replacements we grabbed up anyone, including cooks and headquarters personnel, and threw them into the battle. When the fighting increased, however, these noncombatants panicked and abandoned their heavy machine guns and light artillery pieces without destroying the firing mechanisms. F Company had to fight their way back and disable the discarded weapons to keep them from the Germans.

Just prior to the battle, during our well-earned rest after the Huertgen fighting, we took several trucks and went into the town of Bastogne to find some coal to heat our bivouacs.

While in town we dropped in at a little restaurant for a meal, a pleasure many of us hadn't enjoyed for months. We could see that the restaurant and the other small shops in town were doing business as usual and the customers were mostly workers and tradespeople on their lunch break. Most were congenial and made us comfortable, reminding me of customers in a small cafe at home, though they didn't seem too impressed with our uniforms. They had seen soldiers come and go during the past four years and by now they were more battle-weary than we were.

The chow wasn't that great, mostly cabbage and potatoes with a taste of meat — probably their standard wartime meal but a welcome relief from Army rations. As we ate, we relaxed and began to feel as if we belonged to this group of civilians going about their business in a world that seemed almost normal.

How sad it was to learn several days later that Bastogne had been surrounded by the Germans and in heavy fighting with the besieged 101st Airborne Division, "The Battered Bastards of Bastogne." They fought valiantly at a terrible cost in lives, the town, and probably our little restaurant.

Moving back through the area later we saw evidence of the battle's ferocity. Scattered over a two or three-hundred-acre battlefield were smashed tanks and motorized equipment of all descriptions, and we noted grimly that for every knocked-out German tank there were twenty or thirty of our vehicles burned or destroyed.

The Germans had reinforced their already formidable Tiger and smaller Mark IV tanks with heavy armor plate, which made them nearly indestructible. Looking on the scene I imagined the loss of life that accompanied this hellish battle.

There were large numbers of bodies, mostly German, lying on their backs with snow drifted against them on one side, so they appeared to be wearing grotesque half-masks.

It was here too that I saw my first dead woman soldier, a Polish recruit in the German Army. By now I was used to seeing dead civilians of both sexes, and certainly more than enough dead male soldiers, but seeing this poor dead Polish woman filled me with a great and lingering sadness. I thought then that I hoped I would never see American female soldiers used in combat (though I understand now they see combat on a limited basis).

During the closing days of The Battle of the Bulge our division was assigned to mopping up pockets of resistance left behind after Patton's armored units had swept through the area, ultimately pushing the Germans back behind their border.

Until then I had never been under attack from planes of the German Luftwaffe. Since D-Day the badly depleted enemy air force had been overwhelmed by our fighters and, except for the occasional night sortie, seldom appeared over our front lines.

During the Bulge, the Germans mustered enough planes for an effective low-level attack, and when they came screaming over with their machine guns and cannon firing, I sympathized with the German soldiers under constant harassment from our aircraft.

It is a devastatingly helpless feeling — you think there is no place you can hide or be safe. During a ground attack, at least you can dive in a hole or ditch, but a being strafed by a plane brings a terrible vulnerability. About the only place you could find safety was under the engine of a truck — if you were lucky enough to be near one, or someone hadn't gotten there first.

Toward the end of December the cloudy weather that had been so essential for the Germans' initial success began to clear and our planes were back in the air. Ironically, this created another hazard for our infantry and armor, since the front was still quite fluid and our planes were not always sure where we were.

Infantry and armor worked closely together, the riflemen mopping up around the flanks and taking care of small pockets of resistance. One night it had snowed about an inch, covering up the identification panels vehicles carried on top to be easily identified from the air.

Early the next morning, while we were getting ready to move out with our tanks and other vehicles that had been parked in a narrow street, we noticed three dive bombers circling like vultures overhead. They made one pass to identify us, but since our panels were snowed over, they returned thinking we were the enemy, screaming down toward us on an attack run.

Everyone ran around like crazy, diving into basements and running for cover, and following the old adage: "When in danger or in doubt, run in circles, scream and shout;" until someone with a cooler head thought to leap up on his tank and brush the snow from its topside.

Just in time, the planes dipped their wings and flew off. The tanker's heroic action had saved many lives and much equipment, as these heavily armed planes were definitely coming in for the kill.

My participation in the Battle of the Bulge was that of a common soldier, isolated and sporadic for the most part. I have provided an account of the battle narrated by Col. Gerden F. Johnson, author of *History of the Twelfth Infantry Regiment in World War II*.

The following pages are taken from Col. Johnson's *History*. They are an unparalleled description of the 12th Infantry's gallantry in holding back the massive assault by the German forces.

Col. Johnson was meticulous in his recording of the individual efforts of all the units of the 12th. He names most of the individual soldiers, giving their units and hometowns.

When you read this account keep in mind the personal terror: when he says "lost" visualize the terror of being captured, or killed. When he says "wounded," try to feel the pain of the sudden invasion of a bullet, or a piece of hot shrapnel piercing your body.

Col. Johnson's calm, detached accounts of this battle should not be misread. This was neither a calm nor ordinary event. Even though Col. Johnson saw other intense involvements with men under fire, his description of this heroic stand conveyed personal involvement. I am grateful for his account to reinforce my own observations of men in the front lines.

The pages I have selected deal exclusively with Company F. This is the same company my radio buddy and I delivered the radio to when they were surrounded in the Huertgen Forest. Not only do these pages illuminate my own feelings, they illustrate vividly what happens in the heart of a battlefield.

Company F had first been in the Osweiler area but in the rotation of bat-talions it moved to Berdorf, relieving elements of the 9th Armored Division there. The company command post was set up in the Parc Hotel, a sizeable

building of reinforced concrete. It was three stories tall, besides the basement and attic, and contained many scores of windows. It was located on the road bend 300 yards north of the main junction in Berdorf. The area between the village and the hotel consisted of mainly open fields

THE PARC HOTEL AT BERDORF, LUXEMBOURG

with a few scattered houses.

Lt. John Leake of Keokuk, Iowa employed his entire company (which was only half (strength) on outposts, establishing four. The remainder of the company, consisting of two squads, about 15 men, who were company headquarters, occupied the Parc Hotel.

Company headquarters had telephone contact with each outpost, and with battalion headquarters, also with the 9th Armored Division on the left. A line was being laid to Co. E in Ecternacht, but hadn't been completed. There was no radio communication other than the artillery's sets which were at the outposts. The company scr 300 radio had been damaged in the Huertgen Forest. [This was probably the same radio my buddy and I had delivered to them when they were surrounded by the Enemy, it was beat up already then, now it had been sent back to battalion headquarters for repair.]

Lt. Leake was somewhat concerned about the possibility of enemy action in view of their extremely thin dispositions. What he chiefly thought of a local attack or a reconnaissance in force. He issued orders to all outposts for action to be taken in case they about to be cut off. Outpost no. 3 was to fall back on Berdorf. The other three outposts were directed to retire southward to a battalion at Consdorf in case they were outflanked and in doubt of being able to make it back to Berdorf.

For two days after F Company moved in it was quiet. The fine accommodations of most of the Company, particularly in the hotel, were ideal. On the afternoon of Dec.15, a convoy of 20 wagons manned by several score of civilians approached Berdorf to remove hay, furniture and other things. They were stopped at a roadblock south of the village. Lt. Leake was very upset about this. He felt very uneasy about anyone observing his sketchy defense and wanted to refuse admission. However, a battalion told him the expedition was authorized by division HQ so would be allowed to proceed. The civilians spent some time in town loading the wagons and moved out about dark.

During the night of Dec. 15-16, four flares were reported by observers from outposts no. 1 and no. 2 near the river. They appeared to be on the far side. Battalion headquarters thought that Co. E fired two flares across the river. Nothing else happened until about 0600 on the morning of the 16th, when a heavy barrage fell on Berdorf. A dozen rounds landed near the hotel, however the building apparently was not a special target as the whole town received considerable shelling,

Following this barrage the company found that all its wire lines had gone out. The company commander attributed this to the shelling. A number of sergeants were convinced that Germans had cut the lines. For the next hour it was quiet in Berdorf. There was nothing to indicate that this barrage was a preparation for an attack. The morning patrols were already out when the barrage fell. This left 10 riflemen and the company headquarters personnel at the hotel. The wiremen started out to fix the breaks in the lines. The sudden loss of communications made Lt. Leake anxious to get his radio back. He directed Lt. Mconnell, his executive officer to try to pick it up at Consdorf.

Lt. Mconnell was preparing to go back to the Division Finance office in Luxembourg to dispose of $1,400 in cash along with larger sums of money orders he had been carrying on his person. He and the first sergeant were just getting into the jeep when a man from the anti-tank gun 3 north of town came running up and asked if the company knew anything of the movement of troops south of the Hamm Farm.

At the same time, the company outpost on top of the hotel spotted this movement. At that moment the battalion S-2 , Lt. Anderson, and the S-4, Lt. Finesilver drove up. The S-2 and Lt. Leake hurried to the roof and saw troops in a column of 2's coming down the road from the north. Lt. Leake dashed back down and told Lt. Mconnell and the first sergeant to report the observation as a possible enemy patrol to battalion. Not to forget the radio and hurry back as soon as possible. In a few minutes the fireworks began. Lt. Finesilver decided to go back to battalion to relay the information of what was now realized was an attack of some force. As he wound up his jeep, bullets were flying

"THE BARON'S CASTLE" OCCUPIED BY TEN MEN UNTIL OVERWHELMED AND ESCAPED TO HQ AT CONSDORF.

all around. He drove out of the hotel yard and the town at high speed. As he passed the main road junction in Berdorf, the jeep was fired upon by two or three burp guns at close range. His jeep picked up speed and disappeared.

Now Lt. Leake was in doubt whether or not the jeep had succeeded in escaping. The driver, Cpl. William R. Willauer Jr. of Spartenburg S.C., was hit by five bullets but drove all the way back to Consdorf. Lt. Finesilver also received some bullets through his coat but was unharmed.

The attack closed in rapidly, within the next few minutes the anti-tank squad from gun No. 3 came back to the hotel. Germans coming up the draw from the east had appeared at close range and overrun them so suddenly they were unable to fire. They lost all of their weapons except their carbines. The first ant-tank gun had only armor-piercing ammunition. The 88-mm mortars were lost in the same way. Four of the mortar men came back to the hotel with the anti-tank squad, The remainder got away to the south and reached battalion. The "milk run" patrol came back, having turned around when they saw the Germans advancing.

As the Germans came into town the anti-tank squad on gun No. 2 moved back into the hotel bringing their .50-cal machine gun, having been unable to move their 57-mm gun.

The swift advance of the Germans cut off the outposts. No. 2 and No. 3 were lost entirely. Ten men from OP No. 1 escaped to battalion HQ after an all-day and all-night adventure which is described below. Two men from OP No. 4 made it back to battalion, as did the 81-mm mortar crew. (less the four men who had returned to the hotel). All the rest of the OP's were lost, including the 60 men of Co. F, a heavy machine gun platoon. One anti-tank squad and both artillery observers. All six .30-cal machine guns as well as two of the .50s were lost, also all the mortars and all the .57s.

As the Germans closed in a total of 60 men took refuge in the [Parc] hotel. The composition of this force was as follows:

- *Four officers (Lt. Leake, the platoon leader of Co. H, who had lost his entire platoon except four mortar men; The anti-tank officer, and the battalion S-2)*
- *10 men from the first platoon of Co. F*
- *15 men from company headquarters*
- *4 men from the mortar section*
- *25 men from the anti-tank squads*
- *1 medic*

The only weapon larger than an automatic rifle was the one .50-cal machine gun brought back by the second anti-tank squad.

The Germans closed in swiftly. The men in the hotel saw Germans coming across the main road junction in Berdorf, about 300 yards down the road. This point was fully exposed to fire from the hotel, the rifles and BAR (Browning Automatic Rifle) soon piled up a few German bodies. The enemy stopped trying to cross that intersection.

First Sergeant Willis stood in the window with an automatic rifle trained on the crossroad. Beside him a man with field glasses watched for Germans attempting to get across, and gave him fire-orders. Sgt. Willis claimed that 8 Germans were killed by this method.

The Germans were stopped at the houses and at the cemetery by the fire of the Americans at the windows on that side of the hotel. The lone .50-cal machine gun was taken to the company commander's office and nailed down to the table, with the trail on the window sill, so it could fire on the enemy in the cemetery. There was only one box of .50-cal ammunition, as they were cut off from their supply shed by the Germans.

About 1030 one of the men called to Lt. Leake that Lt. McConnell was coming back bringing a prisoner. They looked out and saw the latter marching up the road from Berdorf with his hands behind his back.

Lt. McConnell had been captured on the return trip from battalion headquarters when his jeep reached the intersection in Berdorf. The first knowledge he had that the Germans were in town when a burst of fire when his vehicle reached that point. Lt. McConnell dove out of the right side of the jeep, the driver, T-5 John Mandicheck of cresson Pa., dove out the left.

Cpl. Mandicheck escaped and was behind German lines for seven days.

Lt. McConnell ran into a building at the corner (a hotel) and kept going until he reached the second floor, hoping he could jump down to the ground from a rear window. He saw two Germans who shot at him. He backed into the room and sneaked to the front window. There he saw about twenty of the enemy shouting at him, one of them fired a rifle grenade through the window. Then McConnell heard them stomp into the lobby downstairs, yelling for him to come downstairs with his hands up. Realizing it was hopeless he walked downstairs. Two of the Germans searched him, taking everything he had, including his watch.

One of them grabbed the money bag containing $5,600 in money orders and currency, emptying the bag on the floor. He and another German began dividing it between them, speculating excitedly about the good time they would have in Paris.

Just then a German Feldwebel (sergeant) came in and bawled the men out. He made them put all the money in the bag and return it to Lt. McConnell, together with his personal belongings. He recognized McConnell as an officer and was correctly polite. He said, "You are my prisoner," almost an apology. He told McConnell he would have to take him to his lieutenant. The non-com then ordered a soldier to take Lt. McConnell to his officer — up there — pointing directly to the Parc Hotel held by Co. F. The soldier directed McConnell to pickup two boxes of ammunition.

Here Lt. McConnell pulled his rank indignantly, claiming that as an officer he could not be required to carry equipment. The German non-com again rebuked the soldier for breach of etiquette. The man then marched the lieutenant off in the direction of the hotel.

The Germans were not aware that American troops occupied the Parc Hotel. The German guard was anything but alert. He allowed McConnell to walk with his hands down, while he carried his rifle in the crook of his arm as if he was going duck hunting. He said they would both have a smoke as soon as they were out of the sight of the sergeant. McConnell decided to disarm him as soon as they got near the hotel.

The Americans inside the hotel watched Lt. McConnell come to within seventy yards. Helpless to take any kind of action, McConnell noticed that the

German was directly behind him. Lieutenant McConnell assumed that maybe the hotel had been captured. When they came within fifty yards a soldier yelled "Is that your prisoner?"

"Hell no, I'm the prisoner," yelled McConnell.

The guard jumped directly behind him, stuck his rifle in his back and said , "Amerikaners, Yah?"

McConnell said he thought so as they were speaking English. The guard then said "tell them not to shoot or I will shoot you." He then marched Lt. McConnell back to the other hotel. He told his Feldwebel that there were two Americans in the Parc Hotel up the road.

The Feldwebel barked an order to his platoon. One squad formed a skirmish line on one side of the road, the other two formed a wedge formation on the road. They started up the road with the Feldwebel and McConnell leading the way.

A few minutes later the Americans saw the Germans coming back up the road, marching Lt. Mconnell ahead of them. Presumably, the enemy squad leader thought the surrender of the Americans was a foregone conclusion. When they were forty yards from the hotel the Feldwebel yelled to his men in German, "Don't fire, we will capture the two Americans."

He turned to McConnell to tell the Americans to come out and surrender. McConnell took the chance the Germans could not understand English and yelled instead. "Everybody, pick a target and fire at the same time."

Then he grinned at the Feldwebel, who grinned back.

Inside the hotel, Lt. Leake gave the command to fire. The first volley killed thirty-three Germans. Several who tried to crawl away were killed. First Sergeant Willils accounted for almost an entire squad with his BAR. Cpl. Hancock shot the German standing behind and a foot to the right of McConnell. Staff Sgt. Colegeo shot the German sergeant in the butt and he fell at McConnell's feet. The Lieutenant put his arm around the Feldwebel's neck and dragged him into the hotel. The rest of the German platoon were dead.

Inside the hotel the German sergeant gave his name and a lot of information on the German's plans for the big push. This information was relayed back to the 2nd Battalion CP with a request for artillery. But mainly, Lt. Leake considered that this was a good time to establish the good treatment Americans gave to their prisoners of war. At this time he thought that his company might shortly be POWS themselves, as they were surrounded. He took care that the German Noncom receive every consideration. He was well fed and given the same cigarette ration as the Americans.

Company F remained isolated for four days, until Dec. 18th when Task Force Standish of the 10th Armored Division arrived in Berdorf. They had two platoons of armored infantry and a company of tanks. They promptly launched an attack on the Germans who were dug in and had a lot of artillery in town.

They were assisted by Company B, who had fought their way into Berdorf several days earlier. They had been sorely depleted in their efforts to dislodge the enemy. They had lost most of their tanks and riflemen. The two combined forces gained only seventy-five yards, but lost twenty-five men and two tanks.

German artillery continued to fall on the hotel, gradually sending the defenders to the lower floors. Many heroic actions by individual soldiers kept the Germans from moving on to their main objective, the City of Luxembourg.

When the 2nd Battalion consolidated its position with the rest of the 12th Infantry Regiment on Dec. 21, Co. F had only 20 men, down from 200 when they were at full strength. But now they, along with all the other companies of the 12th, who had been cut off and isolated for at least a week, saved the City of Luxembourg.

The people of Luxembourg awarded the 12th Infantry Regiment their highest honor, the Fourragere. Every soldier of the 12th was allowed to wear this distinguished award, a gold braided rope and tassel, on the epaulets of their dress jacket.

At this same time the President of the United States awarded the 12th Infantry Regiment the Presidential Citation, a distinctive blue ribbon in a gold frame, to be worn above the left front pocket of the dress jacket. The citation, word for word is the object of the next chapter.

Our sector was the area where the Germans made no useful thrusts beyond our perimeter. Now we were able to chase them back into Germany by leaps and bounds, thus ending their huge counter-offensive.

As the weather continued to improve, we enjoyed the beautiful sight of wave after wave of our planes flying over in pursuit of German tanks and artillery. Until now it had been rough-going for the infantry, which was forced to confront the Germans' massive tanks with bazookas and machine guns. During the battle's early days our tanks had been overwhelmed by the aggressive panzers and German artillery, which for a while allowed the German armor to roam freely and kill our foot soldiers.

But with blue skies and our planes overhead, there was a great feeling of elation knowing the Germans were on the run. When it stopped snowing and the wind died down, the sun shining on the snow made the world look clean and peaceful again.

The sight reminded me of home. After a great blizzard in South Dakota in the '30s, the sun on the snow meant we we could get back to normal living — we could once again care for the livestock and clear the roads and paths instead of wading through the drifts. And I was also reminded of John Greenleaf Whittier's "Snow-Bound." His description of the European winter of 1944-45 was much the same: the weather clear and cold, the snow sparkling, and that same feeling everything being new and clean, and that soon they would be back to normal living.

Now that the German's were retreating, we too could return to normal army living. The kitchens would come back up to the front with hot chow, and we could again select our billets with more attention to comfort rather than safety.

Remember that the infantryman is down at the bottom of the totem pole, expected to do all the dirty and dangerous work with little glamour and sometimes less respect.

I remember one time an anti-tank platoon had been in support of an infantry unit, using its self-propelled guns on some houses where the Germans were holed up and returning heavy machine gun fire.

The fighting went on all afternoon, with the German fire still holding off our infantry, and about dark the anti-tank platoon said they needed to retire to their bivouac area for the night.

Naturally upset, the infantry officer asked what the hell was going on, saying they need them for a final assault.

The anti-tank officer replied that if he didn't retire his men would have to sleep in the field close to the enemy.

"Bullshit!" the infantryman shouted. "What do you think these guys have been doing for months?"

To which the anti-tank officer responded, "That is your job, your men are used to this. Mine aren't."

That, more or less, was the attitude of the rest of the Army: You are infantry and it is your job to take it, as if we were sub-human and loved sleeping in muddy holes in the ground.

If you wish to have even a small insight into the life of a combat infantryman, take the worst day of your life, add sleeping in the mud, eating cold food and being cold and frightened all the time and have someone trying to kill you.

CHAPTER TEN

For the Record

For its actions during the Battle of the Bulge, the 12th Infantry Regiment received not only a Presidential Unit Citation, but the Grand Duchy of Luxembourg's highest military honor, the Fourragere, a braided gold rope with tassels that was worn in the epaulets of our dress uniforms.

The following is the wording of the Presidential Unit Citation to the 12th Infantry:

The War Department in the name of the President of the United States, as the public evidence of deserved honor and distinction, cites the Twelfth Infantry Regiment in General Orders, as follows:

The 12th Infantry Regiment is cited for outstanding performance of duty in action against the enemy from 16 to 24 December 1944. With its weary ranks depleted following a month of bitter fighting in the Huertgen Forest, the regiment moved on 9 December 1944 into a defensive position on a front

12TH INFANTRY
PRESIDENTIAL
CITATION FOR
EXCELLENCE IN
BATTLE OF THE BULGE

extending ten miles along the Sauer River east of the city of Luxembourg, there to rest and await replacements.

At dawn on 16 December, the Germans launched a general offensive against the central portion of the Western Front, implementing the assault to the limit of their resources. The enemy quickly made substantial penetrations in areas north of the 12th Infantry's position, and, as it later became apparent, intended to place the southern shoulder of his offensive squarely within its sector, as he drove to expand south to match his seeming success in the north.

After intensive artillery preparation, which destroyed all wire communications, two regiments of the 212th Volksgrenadier Division were thrown across the Sauer River on 16 December, with the remainder of this division and one additional regiment, reinforced, following on the 17th. At stake was dominating ground and the road net which would open to the enemy the city of Luxembourg, with the 12th Army Group Headquarters, supply installations of great magnitude and Radio Luxembourg.

With crushing weight, the enemy swirled around the defenders, making infiltrations of battalion strength to depths of four kilometers. By nightfall of 16 December, substantial elements of six companies of the 12th Infantry had been surrounded or isolated.

Yet conscious of the imperative necessity of containing the initial drive of the enemy at all cost, this courageous unit held firm. On successive days the regiment was subjected to intensive shelling and enemy attempts to storm the villages and positions to which the determined defenders tenaciously clung.

With great skill and fortitude, the resolute American infantryman disputed villaged, houses by house, and ground, yard by yard, inflicting such fearful casualties that by 22 December the strength of the 212th Volkgrenadier Division had been reduced by one half and its ability to operate offensively destroyed.

At no point had the regimental main line of resistance been pierced. Faithful to its rich tradition, with utter devotion to the task at hand, the 12th Infantry met the critical urgency of the occasion and, undismayed by heavy odds, prevented the enemy from thrusting south, denied him vital military and political installations, seizure and exploitation of which would have grave consequences, and held a position which enabled other units to batter the enemy flank when the heroic 12th was relieved on 24 December.

The courage and fighting determination of each member of the regiment in the stand along the Sauer River presented an inspiring example of the invincibility of free men at arms.

CHAPTER ELEVEN

Into Germany

A fter the murderous frustrations of slugging it out in the Huertgen Forest, and following the dogged defensive fighting during the Battle of the Bulge, it was a great relief to be on the offensive once again, pursuing the retreating Germans across the open terrain of their homeland.

We began to move as rapidly as we had from the Normandy beaches the year before. We rode on tanks and trucks and now fought miles apart from the Germans — who we bombarded with our long-range artillery. We continued at a quick and steady pace, and were stalled only occasionally when the Germans would make a stand and fight where the terrain was favorable for defense.

Riding aboard tanks and trucks was a new experience for me and other infantrymen, and during this kind of fighting — mainly artillery duels between our tanks and the enemy artillery — we ground pounders were now mainly observers, safe for the most part though we were under sporadic enemy fire. We could hardly see the point of attack, which was marked by exploding shells and often several miles away.

And certainly, though the Germans were always dangerous no matter how far away they were, I enjoyed watching the artillery dropping miles in the distance on an unseen enemy. I felt a hell of a lot more comfortable than I had in close combat, with all those mortar shells, small-arms fire and shrapnel whizzing around. For as anyone knows who has been in combat, if the enemy can see you, he has a hell of a better chance of killing you.

By this time the Germans were in desperate straits. They had been badly mauled in their offensive and now were being pursued by ground troops who had overwhelming numbers and resources. And since they had lost control of the air, they suffered from renewed air strikes that had intensified since the Battle of the Bulge.

Being attacked from the air, as I have pointed out, is particularly terrifying since there seems to be no place to hide from a strafing fighter plane. Unlike ground combat, where you don't often see where the shells and bullets are coming from, a fighter plane is highly visible and comes at you in a determined and personal way; as if you were a lowly creature of scorn and humiliation.

Our rapid advance and the luxury of hitchhiking rides on tanks and traveling in trucks slowed, however, as we reached the vicinity of the Prum and Kyll rivers, where we encountered German infantry armed with panzerfausts.

The *panzerfaust* is a German version of our "bazooka," a hand-held rocket launcher highly effective against armor. Understandably, tank commanders feel vulnerable when facing enemy infantry armed with any kind of weapon, knowing that an individual soldier with guts and experience can often disable or destroy his vehicle, and they like to have their own infantry around for protection.

About this time the weather changed to snow and ice. We often had to be supplied by air as the road became impassable. During this time, we lost our battalion commander who was wounded by artillery fire while we were leaving a small town where we had bivouacked the night before. The fire was brought down on us by an enemy observer in a tall church steeple. He was spotted quickly and shot by our men before he could do more damage.

Our present assignment was to clean out the pockets of German troops bypassed by the armored divisions, alternatively relieving other infantry units doing the same and playing "leap frog" to keep up pressure on the enemy. Thus we were in and out of direct contact with the Germans, moving forward steadily, occasionally under fire but seeing a lot of Germany.

Eventually, with a new battalion commander, we crossed over the frozen Prum River through deep snow to take over the first German town to be captured since the Battle of the Bulge. Now on the enemy side of the river, we encountered small bands of German rear guard troops who infiltrated our lines in determined groups that had to be captured or destroyed. Understandably, they fought ferociously, taking advantage of any defensible position to delay our drive into their homeland.

After things quieted down, we were put into division reserve to rest, clean and replace our equipment and further our training. The Army likes to keep you busy and alert, with not much time to think, believing correctly that since your ass has been saved so far, you may be more cautious about saving it for the future.

Having fought us for some time, the Germans by now respected the Fourth Division as a formidable foe, worthy of attention from their propaganda units. Each evening we got a visit from "Washing Machine Willy," a noisy and decrepit observation plane that dropped leaflets during its daily photographic run. These were addressed directly to our unit, the Fourth Division, with its distinctive shoulder patch: a green, spiked emblem with four sides that resembled a cross.

"To the men of the 'Terrible Green Cross,' . . . " the Germans would address their leaflets, following with information that was mostly ridiculous, like warning us of impending setbacks or annihilations. Yet often they contained some information to let us know they knew of our movements or objectives, along with rumors to intimidate or to undermine confidence in our leadership; concluding, of course, with a plea to surrender and "save ourselves."

They also fired propaganda leaflets in artillery canisters, often literally killing two birds with one stone, so to speak. They would fire the shells containing the leaflets, then withhold their fire until we had a chance to pick them up, then follow with their usual saturation barrage. Sometimes they would fool us with a short pause, then resume firing before we could back under cover.

This nasty ploy backfired, however, since we soon began ignoring the leaflets, which were full of so much absurd bullshit it was not worth the risk picking them up, even though the paper came in handy. It all seemed very amusing anyway, since we were right on their heels chasing them back into Germany.

It was during this time that I had some firsthand experience in the making of a Nazi. We had stopped to bivouac in a town of about 40,000, and as usual I was out "fraternizing with the enemy," practicing my crude German while trying to find out how the other half thought and lived.

Next to the house, in which we were bivouacked, lived a very refined and educated woman, the wife of the town's mayor, and her two teenaged children. The children reflected their mother's sensitivity and charm, and despite the brutality of the war and the hardships of occupation, they had retained a realistic perception of all that was happening to them as the war was drawing to a close.

The woman's husband had been mayor before and during the first half of the war, during which time he had resisted local officials who kept trying to get him to join the Nazi Party. He kept them at bay by stalling and telling them he had no political aspirations beyond that of being mayor of the small city. Being quite religious and a devout family man described by his wife as sensitive and caring, he found the so-called "Nazi ideals" morally repugnant.

As time went on, however, the Nazis increased their pressure on the mayor, insisting he take an active part in the party and attend their meetings, ultimately enticing him to attend the great annual party rally in Nuremburg.

After returning from Nuremburg, his wife related sadly, he was a changed man, completely transformed by the moving spectacle of Nazi mass propaganda. His attitude changed, he was no longer as affectionate or sensitive to the needs of his family, and he eagerly awaited his next trip to Nuremburg.

The second trip changed him completely. By now he completely ignored his family, he stopped attending church and alienated himself from his former friends. Eventually he gave up his job as mayor, then left town for Nazi Party headquarters and never returned. Before long, his party loyalty had secured him a position high up in the Nazi regime, having been appointed secretary of all hand labor in the Reich, a job similar to our Secretary of Labor.

According to his wife, who was understandably bitter, he took three "wives," one for social functions, one for a bed partner and a third to bear him more children. This news shattered the mayor's family, to say the least, and the wife found it impossible to understand what had happened to this once devoutly religious family man.

Baffled by all of this, the wife imagined her husband had been subjected to hypnosis or some kind of mind-altering process during his visits to party headquarters that had transformed him into a kind of Nazi fanatic "zombie."

As for myself, I assumed he was converted by abject fear — fear of what they might do to his family or to him personally. By now I had learned that the whole Nazi machine functioned on fear, particularly of the dreaded secret state police, the Gestapo (Geheime Staats Polizei), and the party's ruthless military arm, the SS (Schutzstaffel), which controlled the death camps and, as Hitler's personal army, had complete control over anyone, including some top ranks in the German Officer Corps.

American troops learned of SS cruelty firsthand during the Battle of the Bulge. During the battle a large group of American prisoners were slaughtered by an SS unit near Eupen-et-Malmedy and their bodies left lying frozen in the snow. The incident incited revenge among our troops. The SS must have sensed or expected our vengeance — they fought like fanatics, small SS groups holding up larger American units sometimes for days.

In occupied Europe, of course, the horrors inflicted by the dreaded SS were well known and were partly responsible for the defeat of the Third Reich. The conquered peoples did everything in their power to sabotage the work they did for the Reich, too often as slave laborers, and many allied soldiers owed their lives to the "duds" produced by some French, Belgian or Russian factory workers who had put his or her life on the line.

This great hatred for the Germans, symbolized by the cruelty of the Gestapo and SS, helped create the organized resistance groups that were so effective in destroying communications and rail lines, and other activities that slowed the German war machine.

Which by now, as we fought our way in, Germany showed some signs of abating — though fighting was fierce and often fanatical as we made fast tracks into the diminishing boundaries and resources of Hitler's proclaimed "Thousand Year Reich."

CHAPTER TWELVE

Inside Germany

A s the war began drawing to a close, both sides became a little reckless. For example, while the once powerful Luftwaffe had been reduced to a mostly ineffectual weapon whose planes appeared mostly at night, occasionally some daring Nazi maverick would fly over during the day and strafe us.

These unexpected attacks always scared the hell out of us. Yet whenever the Luftwaffe appeared, we were more at risk from our own machine guns and rifles, as every weapon would blaze away at the plane without regard to where our bullets would land.

As this frenzied fire was scattering shells all over the place, and since most of it was low enough to be hazardous (a bullet fired into the air has the same impact coming back down), those of us not participating in this futile sport quickly crawled into holes.

We always hoped, of course, that the German planes would get hit and quit attacking our position. But they never were, and I don't recall anyone ever been hit from the strafing, though I would bet some were hit by our own wild ground fire.

As we moved into Germany, our accommodations improved considerably. Before, as we moved through France and Belgium, we were usually billeted in barns or other outbuildings, since the Army, in its limited sensitivity, didn't want to inconvenience our allies by moving us into their homes.

But Germany was a whole new ball game. When we were in reserve and not engaging the enemy, we felt entitled to use the private homes of those who were still shooting at us.

Naturally, whenever we could, we picked the nicer homes, reasoning that these belonged to people far up the Nazi ladder, so we had every right to inconvenience them. Not surprisingly, the Germans were usually surly and disgruntled about being displaced, and wanted assurance that we would not take or destroy their finer things.

As you might expect, this assurance was not usually forthcoming from hardened infantry officers, even though there was a strict policy against looting. The Germans, however, who were used to harsh military authority, offered little resistance, though disdain showed through their thinly veiled politeness.

I can still picture those haughty matrons and sturdy hausfraus in their practiced Teutonic stubbornness not wanting to give in, yet knowing their arguments were futile, and finally leaving their precious homes to the fate of the American G.I.

As a rule we did not steal or destroy their property, but quite often were not reluctant to break up their furniture for firewood. Soldiers never seemed to get warm enough. And if we were back from the front or stopped for anytime in a truck convoy, every other truck full of soldiers would start an open fire. These were limited in size only by the amount of time the column was stopped, and the warmth-hungry G.I.s would keep piling on wood (and furniture) onto pyres that sometimes reached a height of ten or twelve feet.

Strangely, this firebuilding mania happened on warm and sunny days as well as when it was cold. The basic need for fire, I reasoned, grew out of our constant lack of the necessities of life. A blazing fire represented hearth, home, warmth and security to the American troops, though by the time the war was over, a lot of German houses were devoid of furniture.

Yet for all this seeming disregard for the property of German civilians, quite often we were more protective of their belongings than their own military. For example, we would give them the alternative of saving towns or buildings of historical significance by leaving or not offering resistance, which, understandably, they were reluctant to do. Hitler, meanwhile, had no such compulsions and was waging war against the civilian population of England with one of his more deadly "secret weapons," the V-2 rocket, or "buzz bomb."

I had first heard these rockets while were bivouacked in the woods near Liege, Belgium, where we were beneath the direct flight path of V-2s headed for London. We knew they were set to come down and explode when their loud buzzing motor cut off, and we were also aware of the tremendous explosive power of these giant flying bombs.

One bright and beautiful day, several of these guided missiles flew over us one at a time, when suddenly we heard the motor cut off one that was directly overhead. This of course sent a panic through all of us and we scrambled for the deepest holes we could find.

The bomb exploded about a half-mile away in open country, yet the concussion picked us off the ground and flung us around like rag dolls. We now realized the enormous power and destructive ability of this weapon, particularly on a huge crowded city like London, where they were inflicting heavy casualties among the civilian population.

Hitler designed the V2s for use against the city of London, hoping that the constant bombardment would make the British want to end the war. By this time, however, the allies were winning on all fronts, and British resolve was indomitable. If Hitler had been more stable, or if he had listened to his generals (which he all but refused to do by this time), he would probably have aimed the rockets at our airfields, supply dumps, troop concentrations and other military targets to gain considerable tactical advantage. Instead he chose to "vent his spleen" on the civilian population of London, and fortunately, through this costly delay, we were to gain a military advantage at the expense of the British people.

Though I can only guess from extensive readings of World War II history, I feel Hitler's main problem with decision making was his stubborn Teutonic mind.

Early in the war, he got away with it. The German Army's huge successes seem to overwhelm any bad decisions by the Fuhrer, who often went against the advice of his generals. If he made a decision he would stick with it, no matter what, even if he was in doubt of the outcome. But as the war turned against Germany, Hitler's megalomania would become increasingly disastrous.

Being German myself, I recognized a common trait of stubbornness among the people I met. For example, I found that many German civilians would invariably get on the wrong side of the house when shells were coming in. I would carefully explain to them that the Americans were fighting their way into town from the west, so the safest part of the house would be on the east side. Then, as we occupied the town, the shelling would come from the German artillery, or from the east, so the safest part of the house would naturally be opposite, on the west side. It was a simple concept, but no amount of explanation in my meager German could make things clear to them.

A farmer I met was going to separate his milk in a cream separator located in a room on the east side of his house, despite the fact that mortar and artillery shells were falling heavily from that direction. While I argued and all but dragged him away, the farmer persisted in plodding through his farm chore until finally it got too hot for me and I fled into the basement. After several hours, when the firing had stopped, I went to check on the man and found that a direct hit had, sadly, wiped out the room, including the farmer.

The very next day, unbelievably, I witnessed another example of German stubbornness: a farmer blithely unloading manure from a wagon in a field where mortar shells were hitting less than two thousand yards away. Both the farmer and his horses seemed blissfully unaware of the danger as he kept shoveling manure as if his very existence depended on it.

I could understand if the man was gathering wood to warm a freezing family, or hunting for food, but hauling manure, even to an old farmer like myself, seemed low on any list of things to do during a pitched battle.

Yet the farmers I met in Germany were older men, of the age that might have witnessed both world wars, and they might have been just sick of the whole thing and said, "to hell with it."

I had already found that the civilian population, especially the older people seemed to accept danger and deprivation with little emotion — as if they had seen it all before, which many of them had.

In fact, I got the feeling they had inherited an affinity with wars down through the generations. For example, their sturdy houses seemed built to withstand military conflict, constructed of mortar and stone with walls sometimes several feet thick, and during an attack they usually lost only the roof and windows.

I always felt sorry for civilians of all nationalities during the war. We had food and adequate support systems, like hospitals and transportation, while they were left to their own ingenuity or the questionable kindness of their occupiers for food and other basic necessities.

Torn from their homes, they trudged along the roads carrying what belongings they could, not knowing if they would find food or shelter. They wandered about with little knowledge of the circumstances rapidly changing around them. They were harassed by war from both sides.

The German people thought we ate quite lavishly. One lady asked me why we ate "cake" every day, referring to our white bread, since they never baked bread from white flour, saving it for cake or other confections.

Ironically, we would gladly have traded some of our "cake" for some their crusty black bread, especially when it was fresh out of the oven. There is nothing quite like slow-baked, thick-crusted dark bread, especially if it is warm and you can get your hands on some fresh cheese and butter.

I remember one time in France, we were stationed next to a bakery a few doors away from a dairy, and for a while we were in G.I. heaven.

Army chow, of course, was at best mediocre. During combat condi-tions,we ate mostly canned or dried K and C rations, but when it was safe they brought up field kitchens so we could have some hot chow and a lit-tle variety, though this was usually as tasteless as the combat rations.

It was difficult and dangerous to bring up field kitchens when we were close to the front. One time the kitchen crew had come up and set out a fairly sumptuous meal on a narrow street in a farming village. As you might expect if you're familiar with Murphy's Law, by the time it was ready to serve, the mortar shells started dropping in. A few brave souls managed to run by, grab some hot chow and dive back into the basement where we found cover. But the rest just sat there in the street all day, aban-doned and uneaten, while we licked our chops and looked out at it hun-grily.

We didn't see a field kitchen near the front for many weeks after that, though we didn't hold it against the cooks. They did the best they could to feed us, especially on special occasions, like Thanksgiving and Christmas. The Army did its best to make our bellies feel at home, and somehow managed to bring us up turkey and all the trimmings for holidays.

Occasionally, we would come upon a trove of foodstuffs unintention-ally left for us by our enemies. One time we had bivouacked in a fine middle-class German home and discovered a well-designed smokehouse in the attic. It was obviously well hidden, as there was strict rationing of food stuffs of this kind, especially the large jar of lard, a precious substance during wartime.

When we brought the lard down into the kitchen, a Polish slave girl working as a house servant plunged her hand into the jar, sighed and licked the lard off her fingers like candy.

Compared to the United States, with its petty wartime rationing of meat, butter and sugar, the situation for most German civilians was extreme to say the least. By this time most were eating mostly black bread, while the luckier ones cooked it with milk in a kind of pudding, which may have been their main meal of the day.

Even though they were our enemies, they were people, and often when we had an extra K- or C- ration we would give it to them, though I never saw them open or eat this gift and supposed they saved it for some special occasion.

Included in our combat rations were some chunks of G.I. chocolate that was hard, dry and not very palatable, but when we gave it to them they treated it like caviar. This often turned out well for us, since in exchange for our chocolate and cigarettes they often dug into their precious hidden stores and gave us some of their best wine.

At this stage of the war, inside Germany itself, we often literally rubbed elbows with the retreating German Army. One evening we were bivouacked in a small town just above a steep hill that led down to a river. From here we had a front row seat on a German unit that was just below us in a flat, partially wooded area. The Germans were doing the things that soldiers do: cooking meals, cleaning weapons, washing clothes and other routine chores.

Directly behind the town was one of our howitzer batteries, which began firing on the Germans. So close was the enemy, that the howitzers had to fire almost straight into the air to lob their shells into the German encampment. Because the sun was just at the right angle, we could see the reflection off these shells as they turned and started their descent, giving us a rare, brief glimpse of artillery in flight, an unusual experience.

We were also in a good position to observe the effects of the shelling on the enemy, which turned out to be a disappointment. All they did was scurry around a little bit faster, completing their chores before finding some holes to escape our attack.

The next morning the Germans were back out in the open, eating their meals and going about their chores seemingly oblivious to the fact that our troops were setting up mortars and heavy machine guns in our positions above them.

For some reason, either because of inexperience or poor leadership, they ignored our preparations. When we did opened fire, they began running around and falling like flies. Our infantry companies followed them, attacking across the river and pursuing them into the woods, and the unusual show was over.

CHAPTER THIRTEEN

Rothenberg

W hen we entered Germany, the primary mission of the American Army was to confront, destroy and force the unconditional surrender of an experienced and tenacious enemy that was fighting fanatically to defend its homeland.

Unlike Germany's other enemies, who had suffered terribly under invasion and occupation by the Third Reich, we were not out to seek revenge, but simply to bring a quick end to a long and devastating war.

Though there were always exceptions, usually necessitated by requirements of survival or comfort, we were not a "savage horde" of looters or pillagers out to ravage the German landscape. And most of us were too tired, dirty and weary of war to do anything but try to get it over with and get home safely.

In fact, as we entered Germany we had been instructed by Army Headquarters to preserve as much of the country's rich history, culture and architecture as we could. This seemed peculiarly ironic when our aircraft were busy bombing Germany's major cities into piles of rubble — or "back to the Stone Age," as a general would say so appropriately in a future war.

Yet as we had experienced, the German Army itself showed little concern for its own landmarks. We kept this in mind as we arrived at the beautiful old walled city of Rothenberg, on the Tauber River; an ancient

cramped and twisted place filled with undamaged medieval gingerbread buildings that made the city seem right out of an old Germany fairy tale.

As we approached Rothenberg, our battalion commander made it known that he would try to spare the

ROTHENBERG, GERMANY

city from an attack planned the following day, and that evening a party was sent through to the Germans asking that they surrender.

Since I was assigned to battalion headquarters, I was part of this historic event. However, for some insightful and rather amusing details of the affair and its participants, I have chosen to defer to the official account witnessed by Col. Gerden F. Johnson, a public relations officer, in his outstanding book, *History of the Twelfth Infantry Regiment*:

"...No, we probably can't wait that long," he said. "I think the doughs'll start moving toward the town tomorrow. But I'll bet the Krauts will be gone and glad they don't have to fight for the place."

Austingen was right, I learned the next morning from Major Burke, the battalion commander. "They have the town already," he said, "and 60 or 70 prisoners. Jumped off at six. There was some opposition outside the place but there wasn't any fighting in the town. Krauts all pulled out or surrendered."

"Think the trip did any good, sir?" I asked.

"I don't know. Guess it did. But we'll never know for sure."

In the morning chow line I met Lichey and we talked it over.

"Well," Lichey said, "if they'd have decided to defend it, a lot of our guys might have been killed. They decided not to and nobody was killed there. I think our trip helped them decide not to defend it."

The First Battalion continued to advance against stubborn resistance and was in position for the assault on Rothenberg at 1525 hours. It was at this time that a Raider patrol of one officer, two raiders, one interpreter and one German civilian were sent into Rothenberg to attempt negotiations for the surrender of the city. The party talked to a German major who explained that he did not have authority to surrender the city, and a detailed account of the experiences of this patrol follows:

At first there were nine of us. Two engineers sat on the hood of the jeep, one of them holding a mine detector. The rest of us were inside the jeep, the driver and two lieutenants in the front and the rest of us in the back. Lichey, next to me, sat on the spare tire and gripped a long wooden pole from which flew a white flag twice the size of a pillow case. We couldn't hear anything except the flapping of the flag as the jeep cruised along the road kicking up a cloud of gray dust.

"Don't have to use that detector now," Lt. Borders shouted to the engineers. "But keep your eyes open, they might have left some of them in the road." Then to the driver, "Take it a little slower."

The jeep crept along the narrow road until we came to a huge shell crater. We got out of the jeep and walked behind the man with the mine detector as he slowly swept a path to the crater. It was deep but the jeep crawled right through it. Then we were riding again. All of us watched the road intently. We passed through riflemen who were walking at about twenty yard intervals and had their rifles slung over their shoulders.

"Good luck guys," one of them shouted to us.

"Hey Lichey, where the hell'd you get that flag?"

The second crater was too deep for the jeep. "Well you guys might as well go back," Lt. Borders said to the engineers. "We'll have to walk in from here." He turned to the driver: "You can take them back with you."

That left six of us. We walked through the crater and up on the road surface again. Keck carried the radio behind Lt. Borders who was holding the receiver to his ear. He was talking to Battalion: "We are about 500 yards out in front of Charlie Company."

"Now keep your eyes peeled for mines," Austingen, the lieutenant said.

"Lichey, carrying the big white flag, walked in the middle of the road and we spread out on both sides of him. Unconsciously we fell into step.

"All we need is a fife and drum and we're the Spirit of '76," Lichey said, laughing. He was getting a big kick out of carrying the flag and he repeatedly refused our offer to take it for a while, even when it became a burden.

We didn't hold step for many paces.

"Hey, hear that?" somebody said. All of us heard it, rifle fire not far ahead of us, quite a bit of it. "If we draw fire," Borders said, "there's nothing we can do but duck and try to get back."

The fire fight grew louder with each step and we began to wonder. It was still going strong as we came within 100 yards of the fight. It was to our right, just off the road. We could see some of the doughs from Able Company, firing around the corner of a farmhouse. Others were running with heads down along a hedge. The Germans were firing from a forested hill almost directly to our front. We couldn't see any of them but they were making a hell of a racket. It was all rifle fire, no machine guns.

"I hope we don't have to walk much farther to find out whether they're going to let us have it or not."

"Able will stop shooting, but I don't know about them Germans."

"Maybe they can't see the white flag yet."

We kept walking and wondering. We were at least partially concealed by tall bushes bordering the road. But as we followed a curve in the road, we must have come into full view, for the firing started to diminish. In less than a minute it ceased entirely. Almost unconsciously we quickened our pace and lengthened our steps.

"Hey look," somebody said, "Here's one of them now."

We were passing within a few yards of a rifleman who had been in the fire fight. He was lying behind a manure pile, rifle nestled in his arms.

"Hey, Pat," he yelled to another dough not far away, "get a load of this." He poked his thumb in our direction.

"Hey!" Pat shouted to us, "Where the hell do you goons think you're going?"

"Rothenberg."

"Well watch out, there's Krauts in that next building. Plenty of them."

We kept walking and nobody said anything. Well, I thought, pretty soon we'll know what they are going to do to us. Almost without noticing it our formation grew tighter, and as each step carried us closer to the house, I stooped slightly and tried to make myself appear smaller. All of us had the same urge, I learned later.

"Keep spread out," Lt. Austingen said. "Won't do any good to bunch up." We spread out, just a little.

"Only thing, they might think it's a trick, that we're sending back information on the radio."

"Well, don't touch the radio, and just keep walking natural."

"Yeah, don't make any funny moves, anybody. These sons-a-bitches probably have their sights on our bellies right now."

"What about the radio? If they fire on us we'll have to break the radio right away."

"No, just change the channel."

"Hell no! Break it; they could find the channel easy. Break it."

We were now close enough to the house to see the window shades. It was a large stone building bordering the shoulder of the road. We would pass within a few feet of the front door. I couldn't see any sign of movement inside the house but I had the feeling it's black windows were staring at me.

"Well, now we know how a clay pigeon feels, heh, heh . . . " somebody said. Nobody else laughed or said anything. The only sound was the flag which slap-slapped in the breeze. As we walked into the shadow of the house, I felt a shiver skiing down my spine the way it does when you think of something particularly embarrassing out of your past. Going past the place, I faced straight ahead, but out of the corners of my eyes I was looking for a place to dive, just in case.

We came out of the shadow into the sunlight again. Nobody looked back, but we could feel eyes on the back of our necks.

Ahead of us the road snaked its way between two hills. "Reminds you of Southern England, doesn't it?" somebody said. From the tree line down to the road the slopes were terraced and divided into small garden plots. An old farmer leaned on a shovel in one of the gardens and watched us intently, apparently unaware that he was taking ten in No Man's Land. On the ridge of the hills to our left a lone figure ducked behind a bush. German artillery observer, we figured.

There was still not a sound from the house behind us but we were still conscious of the place and glad to be getting farther away from it at each step.

Further behind us, we heard the fire fight start up again. "Intermission's over," somebody said. Far off to the right a machine-gun chattered spasmodically. Ahead, everything was quiet.

"How about the major?" Borders said. "Out of the whole battalion he sends for me and says do I want to go? What the hell could I say?"

"Yeh, the old Army system; I want three volunteers. You, you, and you."

"Well," said Austingen, "it will be interesting no matter what happens."

"Think those bastards will fire on us?"

"No, don't think so, not with this white flag."

"You never know about these Krauts though. They might take us prisoners. Depends on what kind of Krauts we meet up with."

"Let's skip it. I keep seeing pictures of my mother opening up a telegram from the War Department."

The sun was strong and we were beginning to perspire. I began to wish I had left my sweater and field jacket behind. We still couldn't see any Germans.

"Have you got it straight now, Lichey, what you're going to say?" Borders asked.

"Yeah, think so."

"What are you going to say?"

"Well, let's see . . ." said Lichey, assuming the stentorian tones of the March of Times announcer. "We are representatives of our division commander. We bring you this offer to spare the City of Rothenberg from shelling and bombing if you agree not to defend it. We have been given three hours to get this message to you. If we haven't returned to our lines by six-thirty, the town will be bombed and shelled to the ground."

"That's it," Borders said. "We want the town and without a fight if possible."

"You know this will be all right if it works."

"Yeah, no use losing a lot of men if you can take a place without a fight."

"What kind of place is this Rothenberg anyway?"

"Oh, it's an old medieval city, I think, built in eleven hundred and something. Lots of art and historical stuff."

"It's got an old wall around . . . Hey! Do you see what I see?"

"Yeah, well pretty soon we'll know."

"Don't use that radio, They'll think it's a weapon."

"Just keep walking natural. Don't slow up."

Not far ahead of us there was a large yellow house built flush against the road. A white-washed stone wall enclosed the backyard. It was very much like the first house we had passed. But this we could see them. At first it was just two black helmets silhouetted above the wall. Then three, and three rifles pointed at us.

"Just keep walking natural," Borders said.

We were within 30 yards of the building when three of them stepped out on the road and started walking slowly toward us. Two carried rifles and one of them had a burp gun. They stopped.

"Halte!" One of them shouted.

We halted abruptly. The Germans looked at each other. They didn't seem to know what to do. One of them finally motioned us on and we walked up to them.

As Lichey was explaining our mission to the tall one a dozen or more Germans came from behind the wall. They formed a ring around us and marched us into the cemented yard and went into the house to get the "commandant."

"See who some of these goddamn bastards are?" Austingen said, jerking his head in the direction of five or six Germans who wore SS insignia on their collars.

"Careful what you call them," Borders whispered. "Some of them may compree English."

Now there were about forty Germans in the yard. I counted seventeen who wore SS insignia. Most of them stopped in their tracks when we entered and were still staring at us. Keck, Grim and I fingered our two-day-old beards self-consciously. We noted that they were all clean shaven, but some were too young to have beards. They were a ruddy cheeked, healthy looking group, except for one thin old soldier with a bullet-creased nose who shuffled across the yard like a man with an advanced case of trench foot.

Finally, the "commandant," a lieutenant, came out and Lichey repeated our mission. Lichey must have spoken German very well, there was a lengthy exchange and they understood each other perfectly.

"What's he say, Lichey?"

"He says he'll have to phone higher headquarters to see what to do. It'll take about five minutes."

"Okay. Tell him that's okay."

They put two guards on us and we walked over into the shade of a small shed and sat down on our helmets. They searched us perfunctorily for weapons and each of us turned in a pocket knife — Made in Germany. They noted the German trademarks and laughed. They had already disconnected our radio and set it aside.

"Funny isn't it," somebody whispered, "to see Krauts this close that aren't prisoners."

"Yeah, they don't look sheepish enough to be Krauts."

"Look kind of scared though, some of them."

"Have reason to be, I guess. Probably be prisoners or dead in a couple of days."

The Germans in the backyard were still watching us closely. Occasionally one or two would drift in, apparently coming off guard. As they entered, they would stop abruptly and eye us skeptically. We wouldn't have attracted more attention if we had just arrived from Mars. Even the old timer and two kids stared goggle-eyed at us from the door of the barn. Only a few of the SS men tried to look nonchalant and uninterested. One group of SS men scowled at us from a distance and made remarks we were unable to hear.

Some of the others came over and spoke to Lichey. Between questions Lichey would translate for us:

German: "Do you have good food?"

Lichey: "Pretty good, sometimes damn good. How's yours?"

German: "Terrible. It is fit for pigs and never hot."

Lichey: "Do you ever get any beer or schnappes?"

German: "We used to get some schnappes but not now. You have plenty to drink, don't you?"

Lichey: "Sometimes a lot, sometimes not any."

One of them came over near me. He pointed to my leggings which were not like those of the others.

"English," I explained, "Anglaise."

He pointed to my shoes. "Gut," he said. He fingered his own black boots which were in need of repair. "Nicht gut," he said, making a face. He explained with gestures that he had walked 200 kilometers in twelve days, that he was tired and had sore feet.

Another German was talking to Grimm who sat next to me.

"Walk you much?" the German asked.

Grimm couldn't resist the opportunity. "Sometimes we have to run to keep up with you guys," he said, laughing. The German didn't understand and Lichey had to do some translating. Apparently the German saw no humor in it.

Another Kraut came up. He was very shy. "What president now?" he asked. The lieutenant stood near us trying to think of something to say.

"Truman."

"Gut?"

"Yah Truman gut."

"Roosevelt gut."

"Ya Roosevelt gut," I said. "Hitler gut?"

"Hitler gut," he said.

Speaking chiefly with their hands, the Germans kept asking all of us about food, drink, walking and other infantry shop talk, even Paris. Some of them used to furlough there. It was almost as if we were members of opposing football teams comparing notes on the rigors of the training schedule and discussing incidents from various games.

They seemed to like and respect Lichey more than the rest of us because he knew the language. They smiled at him and it seemed that they would have trusted him more than us. It had been the same in France and Belgium; if you spoke their language, the local citizens considered you almost as one of them.

The lieutenant came out of the building. He was a hard little guy, solidly built. And old army man, we decided. He spoke to Lichey.

"He says he can get us transportation," Lichey said, "but it'll take about fifteen minutes."

"Good," Borders said, "but we have to be back by six-thirty, you know. Or they shell hell out of this place and bomb it. Tell him."

"What the hell was that?" somebody said, as we heard a sharp explosion nearby. "Kraut artillery, huh?"

"Yeah, Kraut stuff going out."

"Well this is the first time I've been sorry to hear artillery going out."

"When is the war going to be over?"

"As soon as Germany has won it," said the German and he smiled confidently. He really meant it, it seemed.

"Why do you continue to fight?" Lichey asked.

"Why do the Americans and British bring war to us for a second time?"

"Why did you start a war for the second time and make us come over here?" Lichey asked. "Why did you invade Poland?"

At this point somebody asked for a translation. "Better cut out the politics," Borders said. "Can't afford to make them mad right now, you know."

The German wanted to know who would succeed Truman as president. "Tell him it'll be whoever the American people want," Austingen said to

Lichey.

"Ask him who the next Fuhrer is going to be," somebody said.

In answer, the German shrugged his shoulders.

A sergeant came out of the building with an armful of white cloth.

"They are going to blindfold us now," Lichey said. "Vehicle will be here in a couple of minutes."

We stood up and they put cloth over our eyes and tied it tight at the back of our heads. Of course, somebody said something about blind man's bluff. During the first few minutes under the blindfold you didn't feel like a member of a group; you felt alone. Not being able to see what all those Krauts were doing led you to imagine some of the unpleasant things they were preparing to do.

"Hey Borders! You still there?"

"Yeah. That you, Austingen? How about you other guys?" He called off the other names and we were still there."

They led us to the vehicle. The breeze felt good as we rolled through the German countryside. I could see that it was countryside by pretending to scratch the back of my neck, tilting my head and looking down my nose through a narrow opening in the blindfold.

"If someone told my wife I was riding around blindfolded in a German car behind German lines, she's say I was nuts."

"Does feel sort of funny, doesn't it?"

"Wonder how far we're going?"

"Rothenburg isn't very far — if they're taking us there."

"This guy's making a hell of a lot of turns. Hope he knows where he's going. Be a hell of a time to get lost."

There was a pause, the first of many. Occasionally somebody would hum softly, whistle or make an attempt at humor to show he wasn't afraid.

"I was just thinking," one of the lieutenants said, "liquor ration comes in today. That Sullivan will get mine if we don't get back. Bet the so and so's sweating me out."

"To hell with the officers' liquor rations," one of the privates said with a laugh. "But I'd like a swig of something right now."

Another private took up his original thought: "To hell with the liquor ration is right," he said. "If they get it, so should we."

"Yeah, they must think you need a commission to get thirsty."

"Yeah, you've got something there," one of the officers said. "If we get it you should get it or there should be none at all. When we get back, though, everybody gets a drink. We'll need it after this is over."

"We agreed that it was a fine idea.

"Must be going through a town. Hear all those voices?"

"Creating quite a stir, I guess."

"Come to think of it, we must look sort of odd wearing these things."

We had taken our helmets off and sat three-facing-three, with knees almost touching. We were in the back of what must have been a large vehicle with no roof. I tilted my head back and was able to see the roofs of a row of buildings.

"Hey! Do you heart that?" Lichey said. "Somebody just yelled 'schweinhund' at us. A girl I think."

"Literally, it's a dog of a pig."

"Not very complimentary, and here we are trying to save their goddamn old city."

"Well, one thing. So far they are treating us okay. If they were going to do anything to us they'd probably done it by now. I had my doubts about them SS though."

"Hear that? There it is again. Somebody called us schweinhund again."

"The bastards!"

"You know, we still may be on our way to a PW stockade."

"No, I don't think so. Wish we'd get where we're going though."

"The driver's asking directions — There we go backing up again. I hope to hell he doesn't get lost."

"Or run out of gas."

"That's one thing we are doing, using up their gas. They don't have much."

"Say, Rothenburg isn't that far. We'll be beating the Russians to Berlin if we don't stop soon."

"Must be going to corps or army. Probably bump into some Kraut generals."

"What should we do in a case like that, salute?"

"Sure. We salute them just as if it were our own army. It's proper in a case like that."

"I don't like it, saluting Krauts."

"Well, in a case like that it's proper, and besides. . .well . . . "

"Hey Lichey. It must be after five o'clock. Tell this guy we gotta be there toot sweet."

"He says we'll be there in a couple of minutes."

"And how about the radio? We might have to ask for more time. Ask him about the radio."

"He says the radio will be there where we are going."

And somewhat to our surprise, the radio was there when we finally arrived in their little office. The room was crowded, mostly with officers. Some of them looked in from the back door.

The sun streamed in from the two windows causing us to blink and cup our hands over our eyes. It was several minutes after they took our blindfolds off that our eyes became accustomed to the light. Everybody seemed to be smiling."

The Germans were dressed as if they were waiting for a portrait photographer. Their pale green officer uniforms and brass decorations made us look shabby by comparison. But the officers weren't what we expected. Not a monocle in the room. One of them looked like a portly school principal back in Trenton, N.J. Another was the double of a nearsighted medical student I used to know. Just a group of German Babbitts in uniform, but very sharp uniforms, as Keck noted.

We took cigarettes out of our jackets and passed them around. None of the Germans accepted except a private who took one from Keck. He offered one to another private. "No, too young," the German said.

"How old?" Keck asked.

"Sixteen." He looked about fourteen.

Some flunky brought in some chairs and they asked us to sit down.

"Okay, Lichey," said Borders. "Tell him what we want and tell him we haven't much time."

Lichey walked over to a captain and started talking, but the captain pointed to the blond headed major, indicating that he was the senior officer.

Lichey told the major what he wanted. The major asked a few questions, then turned around and started a discussion with the other officers.

"Be sure to tell him if they don't pull out we'll shell and bomb this place to the ground," Borders said to Lichey. "It's up to them if they want to save

this place."

"Yeah, I told him all that."

The major turned around and spoke to Lichey again.

"He says it's okay with him," Lichey translated. "He wants to give up the place and retreat, but he has to get an okay from higher up and that will take some time."

Borders looked at his wrist watch. "It is now 5:52," he said. "Tell him that in exactly thirty-eight minutes this place will be bombed and shelled if we're not back. And tell him I want to use the radio to get an extension of time."

It was all right to use the radio, the major said. Grimm carried it to an open window and Borders started to call battalion. "I have an urgent message for any Pine Station," Borders kept repeating. "Can you hear me? Over." But he was unable to get an answer.

"He says about four hours," Lichey said. "They got communication problems."

"Four hours? That'd be ten o'clock tonight. That's too late. Tell him we can't wait that long. We've got to get back toot sweet or we'll be dodging shells and so will they."

We left the room with the assurance of the major that he was in favor of giving up the city without a fight. For a final answer they wanted us to return at nine the following morning.

"Tell him we will if possible," Borders said as we prepared to leave. We picked up our helmets and somebody came in with our pocket knives we had turned in earlier.

Before being blindfolded again we saluted. The major answered with an American salute but all the others answered with a Nazi salute; "Heil Hitler!" one of them said.

The German who led Grimm and me down three flights of stairs and out to the vehicle spoke English. "American," he whispered. "When will the war be over?"

"Don't know," Grimm said. "Soon I think."

"I hope so," said the German. "I want to go home."

We were permitted to use the radio on the way back. Apparently they were as anxious as we were to stop the artillery, but operating it blind-

folded was a bit complicated, though Borders managed. It was 6:18 when he was finally able to hear battalion and tell them we were on our way.

"Well we don't have to sweat that out anymore," he said. "It's a relief, eh?"

The ride back was short. When the vehicle stopped and we took off our blindfolds we were on the highway near the big yellow building where we had met the first Germans. The two German noncoms who had been on the front seat saluted our officers smartly and sped back to Rothenburg.

The wehrmacht had deserted the big yellow building, we noticed as we passed it. In the backyard there was a cluster of elderly men and women. They waved at us and some of them smiled. One of the women was crying and wiping the tears with her sleeve.

As we left the house behind us, we felt a sudden elation. We were remembering how we felt as we passed it earlier, but we were not yet completely at ease. Lichey held the white flag high as possible. Borders kept talking to battalion.

"They're sending a jeep to meet us at the first crater," he told us.

"Well, it was quite an experience, wasn't it?"

"Yeah, something to tell our grandchildren. Ha!"

"I can hear myself now: "Yes, my child. Your grandfather was behind enemy lines blindfolded for two hours. Only I'll probably make it twelve hours."

"Look! There's a GI," somebody said. A few yards ahead of us a dough was lying on the edge of the road. Seeing him made us feel a lot better.

"Howja make out?" he asked as we passed.

"Not sure yet."

"What the hell's the delay?"

"Okay, go on and fight your way in if you're in a hurry. But if you wait you'll probably get the place without a fight."

Now we could see the jeep waiting for us.

"Looks like they got a bottle too."

"Boy, that's going to taste good. Feel like I been eating cotton all afternoon."

A lieutenant carrying a bottle came out to meet us. We shook hands all around. "Nice going guys," he said, handing the bottle to Borders. "Public relations wants your names and hometowns. Going to do a story on it."

"I'll get the names," I said. "I'm from PRO."

Borders took a long swig of Scotch and passed it around. "Before I forget it," I said, "I better get all your names straight. Give me name, rank and hometown." I wrote them down: 1st Lt. Noble V. Borders, Louisville, Ky.; 1st Lt. Edmund H. Austingen, Hammond, Ind.; Pfc. Herman Lichey, Glendale, Calif.; Pfc. Robert S. Grimm, Tower City, Pa., and Pfc. Peter Keck, Lansing, Ill.

"What do you think will happen?" I asked Austingen as we rode in. "Think they'll hold up so we can go back tomorrow?"

"That's the way Lichey and I figured it out. But you never know for sure about things like that."

In official reports the action stated that patrols from Company C entered Rothenburg at 6:30 on the morning of April 17, and the company subsequently reported that Rothenburg was an open city because of the many hospitals there. Request was made that artillery falling on the outskirts of the city be lifted.

Later, Companies A and C advanced through Rothenburg without encountering any resistance.

CHAPTER FOURTEEN

Entering Rothenburg

During the evening the surrender party entered Rothenburg, I was on the radio in the command post of First Battalion where I was literally tuned in to what was going on.

From listening to comments by Lichey and Borders, I was able to discern that the German officer commanding Rothenburg was limited as to what he could do. German communications had broken down and there was a danger that any agreement might be rescinded once communication was restored.

The German commander did agree, however, to pull out and take positions behind the city, but warned that if he received orders to defend Rothenburg that's exactly what he would do.

I was not privy to the final decision from the battalion commander, Colonel Jackson, as I went off shift before the decision was made. So I will give my impression as to what happened next. This will also explain my fears on the next morning's happenings. I did not know that two of our companies had already cleared the town.

Skeptical of the situation, our battalion commanding officer decided to send a small group into the city the next day to check things out. The party was kept small so as not to alarm the Germans, who might have offered resistance to a larger force, and to make it more convenient for any negotiations.

I was assigned as radio operator to the party. Since I had monitored all the radio traffic from the evening before, I was also more than a little nervous, figuring there was a good possibility the Germans might decide to put up a stiff fight.

As we moved up to within shooting distance of the walled city's huge gate tower, I could visualize that tower as being a perfect spot for a machine gun, and I remained apprehensive right up to the point where we walked through the gate and into the town.

Inside the gate we were somewhat surprised to be met by a large crowd of civilians, and though there was no opposition, I remained nervous as hell so that my hand shook as I tried to light a cigarette while holding onto my radio handset at the same time.

Seeing that I was doing a poor job of both, a German soldier came out of the crowd

GATE TO THE HISTORIC CITY OF ROTHENBERG, GERMANY. APRIL 1945

and lit my cigarette. When I said "Danke" in German, he seemed as relieved as I did, explaining that he had been wounded and was home on injury leave. When both sides saw us smiling and carrying on this casual conversation, everyone began to relax and breathe more easily.

Though there was only a handful of us, the Germans seemed compliant, if not friendly. Soon we located the mayor and gave orders that all weapons be turned in, and within a very short time people were bringing in all kinds of stuff to Rothenburg's Rathaus, or city hall, where it was deposited in a heap on the floor.

It was a weird collection of weapons, indeed. There were old and very valuable hunting rifles with carved cheek pieces and engraved barrels; handguns of all kinds, some of them obviously homemade, in addition to knives and other dangerous looking implements that seemed to belong in an arms museum.

I was particularly impressed with a German officer's sword, a beautifully crafted and expensive looking weapon whose blade was lavishly engraved and whose handle was adorned with a Nazi eagle, globe and swastika, all in gold. The sword was attached to an attractive green leather harness obviously designed for dress occasions, and I chose this and a Nazi flag someone had taken down from above city hall for my personal souvenirs.

The huge red flag was about twenty by thirty feet, with a ten-foot black swastika in its round white center. I stashed this and the sword in a closet where I was working. Unfortunately, these were later stolen, probably by one of the   rear-echelon bastards who had entered Rothenburg as soon as they knew it was safe.

I was sure it had to be one of them, because no front-line soldier would steal from another of his buddies. The rear-echelon bastards were always looking for souvenirs, though by the time they reached the front

anything worthwhile was gone. After I was relieved from duty, I grabbed my carbine and went looking for my stolen property. I don't know what I would have done if I'd found the guy, so it was probably a good thing I didn't.

Soon after, we left the town in the hands of our occupation forces (which probably included the son-of-a-bitch who stole my souvenirs), and moved on.

(Years later, in 1967, my wife and I visited Germany and made a special trip to Rothenburg, a quaint and picturesque little city whose preservation, I pointed out somewhat proudly, had been the result of our GI diplomacy nearly twenty-five years before.)

Shortly after the occupation of Rothenburg we returned to combat, moving rapidly across the fields of Germany and back quickly into danger.

Late one evening we entered a small farming community, where our colonel established a battalion command post on the ground floor of a farm house. The house was next to a church on one side of the village square, and from there the colonel was trying to get better communications with his front line troops, who were set to attack the next day.

To get better reception, I had set my radio on a window sill with the antenna pointed outside. It was quiet and the room was dark so I had no worries about parting the blackout curtains. To better use the radio's handset, I had also taken off my helmet.

Just then, happening quickly and unexpectedly as things do in combat, a mortar shell exploded against the church steeple next door and I felt shrapnel cut into my bare head.

Stunned for a moment, I looked behind me and saw that some bozo had briefly lit a lamp in the room drawing enemy fire. The lamp was quickly put out, and I got my helmet back on, but by then I could feel a trickle of blood dripping down my face and neck.

After the blackout curtains were replaced, the lamp relighted, everyone was staring at me and urged me to go back to the battalion aid station. Knowing that even superficial scalp wounds bleed like hell I refused, reluctant to travel back over a road that was exposed to enemy fire. I didn't feel that bad and wasn't worried about the bleeding.

However, I guess I protested too much, because my buddies thought anyone who didn't want to go back to rear must be suffering from a concussion, and I was sent on my way. We made it safely, with only a few misses from enemy shelling, and the sergeant who went with me woke the duty doctor so he could examine me.

The doc checked me over and asked a lot of questions that I thought were unnecessary, but, as I learned later, were to establish my eligibility for the Purple Heart medal. After that, the doc shaved my head, sewed me up and I was given light duty for a few days.

Later, when I received the Purple Heart (along with the Bronze Star for bravery, which I felt I really didn't deserve), I felt I had earned the Purple heart since I had sustained injuries from direct enemy fire. But he Bronze star was another matter, as I couldn't justify any bravery to the act of just carrying a radio to a surrounded company that had it one hundred times as tough.

PURPLE HEART
AWARD FOR BEING
WOUNDED BY
ENEMY ACTION

BRONZE STAR
WITH OAK LEAF:
2ND AWARD FOR
HEROIC SERVICE

When I returned to the front, I found myself in a farm yard where our troops had been engaged in a vicious firefight the day before. Once again we established our command post in a farm house surrounded by some outbuildings. A hot chow line had been set up there, which was a welcome surprise this close to the front.

Looking around the barnyard, I noticed a low, wide pile of what I thought was manure, over which was spread a lot of blankets. Some men were sitting on the pile eating, and I figured some sensitive soul had covered the manure during mealtime.

Just then, however, a Graves Registration unit pulled up and uncovered the "manure pile," revealing a stack of corpses they began to toss into the back of a truck. Since hot chow was hard to come by, some of the guys just wandered off a few feet and continued eating. Others, though, couldn't take it and one guy puked his guts out.

I thought this was a bit callous of the "body snatchers," particularly at lunch time. But they were in a tough business, used to collecting bodies in all kinds of condition, and by now they were pretty well conditioned themselves.

By now the front line was moving at a rapid pace, so our next CP was in a remarkably incongruous environment: the large and lavish summer home of some well-to-do German we presumed was a high Nazi official. We hadn't yet seen this kind of elegance. The place was full of marble-topped tables with gilt legs, elaborate chandeliers, tapestries on the walls and beautiful paintings everywhere.

What impressed me most, was the view. From a large room on the third floor was vast and splendid view of the Bavarian Alps. In the same room were a number of well-executed scale models of official buildings of the Third Reich, including the cultural center at Nuremberg.

One of the female servants, a Polish slave girl like the one I'd encountered before, told me in German that the home was owned by a high-ranking architect for the Reich. After the war, I wondered if it might have been that of architect Albert Speer, who was Hitler's minister of war production.

Thanks to a group of fanatic young SS troops holding up our advance, we stayed in the home for several days. The SS was Hitler's elite Nazi army, and its soldiers were highly trained and politically motivated, and often fought harder and caused us more trouble than regular German Army units ten times their size.

By this stage of the war the average Wehrmacht soldier was in his forties, some even much older, and unlike much younger SS, who often fought fanatically to the end, they were also much wiser and now giving up in droves, recognizing the war as a lost cause.

Even I could tell it was a lost cause, and it became apparent one day when I and another radio operator "captured" one of these worn and weary old German soldiers.

We were in a jeep going over a hill when all of a sudden this middle-aged German soldier began waving at us frantically. He was unshaven, dirty, his uniform tattered and torn, and he looked less like a soldier than some old wino back in the States. I think we stopped more out of pity than anything else. But in the best textbook style we made him put his hands over his head, and I quizzed him casually in broken German as we drove back to our battalion CP.

When we arrived, the German, unafraid and by now an old friend, was lounging comfortably in the jeep smoking an American cigarette, sighing to himself and expressing gratitude for being in our hands.

Our capture of this "fierce Nazi superman" brought us a lot of ribbing for days to come.

CHAPTER FIFTEEN

Bits & Pieces

hen the war finally ended a few months later, I was surprised to find myself experiencing a great let down. I was relieved, of course, as all of us were who had not been killed or seriously wounded, but overnight we were left with an indefinable void in our lives.

Soon we would be civilians, but we would never be the same. Never, for as long as we lived. For the camaraderie of men in combat is exclusive and it closeness goes beyond whatever you might expect from friends or even family members. You eat, sleep, fight and face death with them. You share whatever you have, from cigarettes and shaving cream to dry socks and money.

I once had a three-day pass to Nancy, France, but no money. Yet when my buddies found out and I got ready to go, I suddenly had more money than I knew what to do with. Later, while I was spending all that dough in Nancy, I realized that they had bought the goodtime stories I would tell when I returned.

Actually it was difficult to spend all that money in Nancy, but we gave it the old college try. There were shows to attend, with accomplished musicians, actors and actresses. They did mostly musical numbers as I think they knew us GIs, and a quite few civilians could not understand French. Of course there were all those glitzy bars. In the States, if a GI went into a bar (we usually picked the better ones), the patrons would not let you spend your own money, knowing you were only making 21 dollars a month. Also, many of them felt guilty for still being civilians. Some good shares of them were just downright generous.

In Europe the situation was reversed, we probably had more money than the civilians so there were very few free drinks. Of course there was always ample opportunity to spend a bundle on the girls, which is what most of us came for.

After this diversion from our troubles, even for such a short period, we had a chance to reflect on combat situation.

There is no experience in life that can prepare you for life in combat. Absolutely nothing in civilian life duplicates the hellish conditions you experience. You are always under some kind of harassing fire from mortars, artillery and small arms. Yet strangely, the enemy fire is not your major concern — you just learn to live with it.

No, the outstanding legacy of war, is the primitive living conditions. I could never get used to them, even as a former farm kid from a hard-scrabble life in South Dakota. Most of the time your clothes are wet and always dirty. There are long periods when you can't shave or even wash — which was most apparent on the faces of the dead.

The dirt on the faces of the dead appeared to be an extra layer transposed onto the transparent gloss of their own lifeless skin. This illusion left me with an extra measure of horror mixed with compassion, knowing a person had to die this way — without the basic and decent amenities of warmth and dryness.

Being scared happened only once in a while, and you could only die once, but the supreme insult was dying dirty and cold without any family around. Seeing dead men in combat, I could never stop thinking about what must be man's ultimate loneliness.

I feel it was the living conditions rather than the danger, that drove some men to wound themselves. I knew of two soldiers who shot themselves to get away from the war, or at least the front, and it happened while were in a relatively safe area, but where conditions were the most horrible I'd ever experienced.

One man shot himself in the foot while in his foxhole. He had been despondent for a while, and the act was like a mini-suicide, with each having the same cause, we would learn. We never learned what happened to the man, in fact we didn't want to know. But we hoped he would get no punishment since by now, we all could understand how a soldier might break.

The other man invited a "million dollar wound" by sticking his hand up out of his foxhole during heavy fire, something my buddies in the radio section accused me of, jokingly, whenever I volunteered to go up to the front line.

In the Huertgen Forest, getting wounded to get out of that unbelievable hell hole was about all we talked about — and no one was sure whether we were joking or not. In that battle some men in battalion headquarters were wounded, though we were considered to be ten times safer than the men in the line companies.

A soldier's first wounds, if not extremely debilitating, usually put him into a euphoric state. He realized that being wounded wasn't as shattering an experience as he had anticipated. Also, it was a temporary way out of a difficult situation. He knew he would soon be in a rear area with dry, clean clothes, a warm bed and hot food for a while.

Mostly, though, he knew he had survived his baptism of fire and had come out better than he expected. Even some men I saw with serious wounds felt this way, though I saw them early on, when they were still numb from shock and filled with morphine.

Even more depressing than the physically wounded, were those suffering from combat fatigue or "shell shock." On several occasions I saw these men on visits to the battalion aid station. It was heart rending to see big strapping men break down and weep. Many wept because they felt guilt at leaving their comrades in a tight situation.

Those suffering from shell shock were taken off the line because of their inability to function normally. Often they just sat and stared vacantly while artillery fell all around them. Others might wander off into areas of danger, in mine fields or toward enemy lines; uncaring, as if their bodies were rebelling against the horror around them (which they were, actually).

By the time these shell shock cases were brought into the aid station ,they were in a world all their own, having shut out everything around them. Watching them, I could only hope that their imaginary world was more pleasant than the one the rest of us still lived in. And if so, I could envy them their escape from the war.

I always wanted to help but didn't know how or what to say. Maybe I would offer them a cigarette or K ration, and sometimes I'd get a slight response. But I never knew if I was giving them any comfort since they were usually taken away before I could get anything out of them. This always left me feeling a little bit lost myself.

From my limited observation, it was usually the more refined and sensitive men who would break first, while us dumb farm kids held our own a bit better. But this may have been a minor prejudice I formed, since I seemed to handle the pressure better than most.

It is difficult to assess how much pressure a man can stand, or what would provoke such extreme fright in a combat soldier. I know that in my first combat mission, I was a good example of how naive a person can be until he has faced enemy fire.

I learned quickly, after being blown off my feet and into a hole, that you could not wait for the explosion to hit, but had to listen for the gun to fire and the whistle of the shell on its flight. Soon, I was constantly listening for the faint sound of a shell in flight so I would had enough time to get down or in a hole.

The bigger guns and mortars gave us more time, but the German "88s," anti-aircraft guns used on tanks and as artillery, were nasty weapons. They fired shells so fast, you only had seconds to get out of the way.

As far as officers were concerned, combat usually made good ones better and bad ones more compassionate. Many times when a line officer came to the command post for briefing, their main concern was for the troops and how to ease their situation with fewer casualties. Many would do anything, including putting themselves at greater risk, to spare their men. There were several instances during the Huertgen Forest campaign when commanders chose to be relieved, rather than throw their men into impossible situations.

In the Huertgen Forest there were so many officers lost, that battalion headquarters often sought volunteers from the ranks for battlefield commissions. I didn't know about the others, but I felt my lack of leadership ability and poor knowledge of infantry tactics would have done more harm than good. Others declined for much the same reasons, and to be honest, most of us would rather stay at battalion headquarters than risk getting our butts shot off in a front line infantry company. As I've said, I had no fear about going into combat and did so often, but I went in as a private soldier, not as a second lieutenant, whose mortality rate was among the highest in the Army.

Then, too, there was the underlying thought that these promotions should come from within the line companies themselves.

In retrospect, the better officers and non-coms, especially those with many men under their command, often placed themselves in danger to assure the safety of their troops.

I was particularly sympathetic for the company commanders I saw arriving at night for briefings at our battalion command post. These men had to come long distances, often under heavy mortar and artillery fire, and in the darkness had to occasionally dodge shots from our own jittery men.

CHAPTER SIXTEEN

Aftermath

Up until now our war had been one mainly of survival, staying alive while killing the Germans as quickly and efficiently as possible. One day we were reminded of the greater, almost forgotten purpose in our being there as we passed near the infamous Dachau Concentration Camp.

As we drove along in trucks to a new assignment, we were suddenly mobbed by hundreds of newly freed, terribly emaciated men dressed in filthy prison stripe uniforms. They swarmed over us, trying to embrace and kiss us, hysterical and overjoyed to the point of ecstasy, unaware that we were not their actual liberators.

The unit that had liberated the camp was well down the road from us, but I think it took these people some time to recover from the shock and initial disbelief of their good fortune.

We learned that the Germans had planned to kill them all to leave no witnesses to their atrocities. These poor devils had lived for some time not knowing if they would be gassed and burned or simply left to starve to death. All they knew was that their oppressors had gone and the gates of hell had suddenly opened.

Seeing them, we felt huge and overfed by comparison. There were feelings of pity of course, but also the embarrassment of knowing it would be presumptuous for us to even attempt to interpret what they had been through.

It took hours for us to get through these deliriously happy prisoners who crowded around our trucks for miles. I knew that the officers just ahead of us were impatient to get going and get out of there, but they made no move to break up this spontaneous and emotional demonstration.

Everyone was moved by the mass outpouring of gratitude. Many of us hardened combat veterans had tears in our eyes as we observed what we knew was a once-in-a-lifetime spectacle. We felt privileged to be able to see the relief and joy on the faces of those who had survived.

Yet we were only seeing the survivors. Those who had liberated the camp had seen the horrors firsthand: the piles of bodies, the ovens; the mud and wire and barracks of the most terrible act of inhumanity in modern history.

The poor prisoners wandered about without knowing where they would go, and probably didn't even care. All they knew was they were free and it was suddenly too much to handle. I tried to put myself in their place, but it was difficult to imagine what they had been through. Since we were moving on, there was no way we could examine the camp. But I imagined the simple joy they would feel that night to sleep out under the stars, rather than their cold, dark and smelly barracks. They were finally free, but did not know where they would be tomorrow.

We were fat and happy over the war's end and would soon be returning to a peaceful and prosperous America. There was nothing in our past experience that could duplicate the horrors these men had suffered under years of Nazi murder and brutality — never knowing, and eventually probably not even caring which day might be their last.

Their faces radiated all the good things that could or would ever happen to them, and it was though we had given them all their favorite holidays and anniversaries rolled into one.

When time came to move on, it was very difficult to leave that joyous scene. We talked about it among ourselves afterwards and it suddenly came into focus — we realized that much of what we had been fighting for was there behind us, standing alongside the road cheering, crying and reaching up to us. It was a very humbling moment.

With the war over, we moved quickly and easily into defeated Germany and began to operate like victorious troops in other wars, foraging for food and booze where we could find it. We had ample K and C rations, so unlike hungry foragers in other times, notably our own Civil War, our foraging was based less on need than greed.

We were all hungry for fresh foods, especially eggs, milk and meat, and we soon discovered that these were often plentiful in supplies reserved for the German officers'.

When we got our hands on something like fresh eggs, which we all craved, we went hog wild. I remember us eating several dozen each one day — boiled, scrambled and fried, both over-easy and sunny-side-up. The six men of our radio section alone ate the better part of two cases (60 dozen eggs) in just two days.

But hell, we were all young and in great shape — and certainly no one had ever heard of cholesterol in those days.

It was difficult to say which was higher on our list of priorities, fresh food or booze, but I guess it depended on the mood at the time. Needless to say, coming upon a cache of German officers' alcoholic beverages, as we did one day, was always good for our morale. The officers had the good stuff: hard liquor, wine and even some champagne. We loaded cases of the stuff on a liberated German Ford flatbed truck.

At this point things were getting a little raggedy ass, and while we were supposed to fall in behind the rest of the regiment, by now moving quickly through German territory, we got a late start and began to straggle behind. The old Ford wasn't running very well, and before long we found ourselves so far behind we were losing radio contact, which eventually we did, giving us the excuse we had been looking for.

Hell, we knew where everybody was going anyway, and we could catch up anytime we wanted to, but we wanted to relax and have some fun. So for two glorious days, the six of us became our own little unit "somewhere in Germany," operating on our own as if we were no longer in the Army.

As we roamed about, drinking, sightseeing and generally having a good time, we didn't even have to touch our more than adequate supply of booze, which we had stacked in cases three deep on back of the old truck. The "natives were friendly," as the saying goes, surprising us by bringing out their best wine and sometimes even their powerful schnapps. We shared our rations with them, they gave us their delicious black bread, and we all ate and drank and said "to hell with it."

Though we were deep into Germany by this time, the people often surprised us by treating us as liberators, especially in the rural areas. There, the farmers and small town folks were less politically motivated, and many saw the Nazi philosophy as oppressive and were glad to see the whole business coming to an end.

You have to remember, of course, that it was probably the more liberal-minded Germans who came forth, while I imagine the diehards were less eager to mingle with our little safari.

Yet for the most part we were treated as friendly visitors instead of the enemy, and in those two short days we made some intense friendships. I particularly remember a school teacher from Vienna who had the most beautiful soft accent when she spoke English. When I complicated her, she explained that Americans pronounced their language too harshly, which is why English sounded softer and better when spoken by other nationalities.

When I asked what she was doing in Germany, she explained she had left Vienna and a lucrative job to get away from the Nazis, who were not as predominant in the rural communities.

After two pleasant days we decided we'd goofed off long enough, and after some tinkering to get the old Ford running better, we said our good-byes and hit the road with our load of booze to catch up with the regiment.

When we finally caught up with our outfit, our officers, much to our delight, put us in charge of our truck and its load of booze, which was like putting the fox in charge of the henhouse. The deal was, we were to make an inventory of the various kinds of potables stacked on our old Ford and make them available to other platoons and sections. Needless to say, the better stuff somehow never made our inventory list, leaving the radio section with a more than ample supply of champagne and fine wine, while the rest of the troops got what was left, some of it barely drinkable.

I have to admit, the radio section represented the biggest bunch of boozers in the whole company, and we were always on the prowl for some kind of drink or other. One time we found ourselves in a bombed-out liquor store. After sampling everything in sight, we were disappointed by what we had found. In Germany there was a wide difference in the quality of booze, from undrinkable to WOW!, and we realized that other troops had gotten there before us.

Snooping around, however, as persistent boozers will, we uncovered a small case of schnapps buried beneath rubble and snow. This, we found, was in the WOW! category, and we quickly filled all our canteens and headed back to our bivouac.

Along the way, we stopped and shared what we thought were sips of this superb schnapps with everyone we met. The stuff was ice cold, naturally, so as we drank our mouths and throats were anesthetized and it was hard to tell how much we were drinking.

By the time we got back to our bivouac, however, several of us were beyond "happy," and the last thing I recall that night was reaching for some beautiful french-fried potatoes some thoughtful soul had made.

I woke up the next morning with the daddy of all hangovers, and almost frozen to death. That was the first and last time I got drunk while overseas (not a good policy, especially in a combat area). For months afterward the mere smell of alcohol could make me sick, which was a lousy state of affairs when I was still so closely associated with that bunch of boozers in my radio section. Every time someone popped a cork, I had to leave for danger of puking my guts out.

CHAPTER SEVENTEEN

Heading Home

S oon after the war ended, during six glorious weeks that would have been the dreams of any battle-weary G.I.. We were billeted in a surprisingly comfortable German castle that had been owned by a nobleman of some sort and was called "Schloss Schwartzenberg" — In English, "The Castle on the Black Hill."
Schloss Schwartzenberg dominated a hill overlooking a small town — "Sheinfeldt Um Schloss Schwartzenberg" — and was surrounded by the owner's private hunting grounds, the "Steigrwaldt."

Unlike castles I had experienced before and since, huge, drafty old rock piles that seemed barely livable, this was a large two-story building that seemed fairly modern by castle standards.

Actually it was a complex of buildings: a set of servants' quarters that extended some two hundred yards from the main building, stables and tack rooms opposite across a wide courtyard. Attached to the end of the stables, we discovered after snooping around, was a large ice house and brewery that got our immediate interest.

As I've said, we were a hard-drinking outfit, and it was our good fortune to find the castle's brew master still hard at work and keeping a close eye on two huge vats of fine quality beer. This he bottled the old-fashioned way, without carbonation, and it made a superb drink, hearty and thick, with a good taste of hops that

"SCHLOSS SCHWARTZENBERG" — THE GERMAN CASTLE WHERE HAROLD STAYED ON A REST IN 1944.

reminded me of the home brews we made during Prohibition.

With our own brewer and other servants keeping the castle clean and in repair, we were living high on the hog. We even had German prisoners of war to cook and do the dishes, so the only regular duty we had was guarding the castle and our prisoners. Though God knows they would never try to escape since most hadn't eaten this in a long time.

I occasionally guarded these guys when they were off duty and it gave me a chance to try out my fractured German. They thought was funny as hell when I screwed up the sentence structure. Most German sentences are arranged backward from English, like: "He threw the cows over the fence some hay," so you can imagine their hilarity.

I had never learned the language, just a smattering of German words and phrases from my grandmother when I was a little kid. She would speak German to us and we would answer in English, which she understood but had difficulty speaking properly. When I explained this to the POW's, they were sympathetic and helped me to sort things out and soon I got pretty good at simple, everyday conversations.

Since we were out of the war now and just biding our time, the castle became a kind of rest camp and was a delightful place to explore and snoop around, especially for a kid from South Dakota who had more imagination than good sense.

One evening at dusk I was poking around the castle grounds when I discovered a hidden, sloping wall that appeared be a buttress holding up one side of the massive building. In the wall was a heavy door none of us had seen before. I opened the door and found myself looking into a dark and gloomy space that seemed to be used for storage.

As my eyes gradually became accustomed to the darkness, I was startled by a group human figures. A castle is a spooky sort of place at best, so I was frightened by this weird spectacle and felt the hair raise on the back of my neck. I didn't know if I had stumbled upon some ancestral ghosts, a secret meeting, or maybe the rumored "secret underground," who were frozen after being found in a place where they shouldn't have been.

I felt foolish being scared, especially after all the combat I'd been through. After I left (rather hurriedly, I admit) I decided to return with a flashlight to satisfy my curiosity. I returned by myself, not wanting any of my buddies to think I'd flipped out and was seeing ghosts,. When I crept back into the room my light caught a group of figures made out of wax. They were remarkably realistic, and when I returned later with the guys from my unit, we examined them more closely.

From what we could guess, the figures were those of the people important to the life and times of the castle, probably past barons, knights and whoever, arranged in a kind of formal tableau. Looking into their eyes, which were real as hell, they seemed aware that we were enemy invaders who had bumbled into their sanctuary, and I think I would have preferred seeing a ghost.

During our stay at Schloss Schwarzenberg we began to feel at home in the surrounding countryside, which had a lot of small villages scattered around, surrounded by hills and forests, and seemed to have suffered little damaged from the war.

Now that war was over, we also had a lot of free time to goof off. As spring turned into summer, the sap began to rise in our horny young bodies. We often left the castle and enjoyed strolling through the castle's forests. To our delight, we soon discovered young village maidens liked to stroll through the woods and sniff the fresh country air.

Not to beat around the bush, so to speak, we soon developed "intense friendships" that quickly spiced our pleasant, but cloistered lives at Schloss Schwarzenberg. A buddy and I began double-dating two of these maidens. Though neither could speak the other's language, the couple fell head over heels in love. I helped translate some, but they managed quite well through the universal language of love.

Though my proficiency in German was barely first-grade level, there was a guy in my outfit, a wiseass sergeant from New York, who accused me of chatting up the Frauleins and taking them all for myself; which was bullshit because I was constantly setting up guys in my platoon.

One day the sergeant tried to pull a fast one. He told me he wanted to introduce me to his new girlfriend. Since she spoke English, he said, there was no need for me to interpret and I would have no influence over her, an accusation I thought was a little strange. I was puzzled, and wondered why he would want to introduce me anyway.

A few days later he brought her around and I saw why. She was a very lovely young woman and it was obvious he wanted to show her off. We quickly struck up a conversation in German while the sergeant looked on proudly, a large smug grin on his face.

After some polite introductions she got right to the point: "You seem like a nice fellow . . . unlike some people," she said sharply, turning her head and smiling up coyly at the beaming sergeant.

"I think New Yorker's are crude," she added bluntly, then surprised me by getting right to the point. "I wonder," she asked sweetly, "if we might see each other sometime soon?"

Then we all smiled again, and the sergeant, who now had his arm around her and was still beaming smugly, asked eagerly, "Well? What did she say?"

I nodded to the woman, and after thinking for a moment, enjoying the look on the sergeant's face, said, "She says she has very good taste in men."

As it is in the Army, however, we soon had to leave the village maidens and Schloss Schwarzenberg behind, having received word we would be transported to the port of Le Havre, France, where we were to embark for the States. While normally we would have been jumping for joy, we also learned that our unit was being moved on a priority basis. Once back in the States we were to retrain with our division and prepare for what was predicted to be a costly invasion of the Japanese home islands.

The war in the Pacific was still going hot and heavy, the Japanese were putting up a hell of fight and not about to surrender. At this point, we'd all heard of the atomic bomb that would end it all by August (1945).

When they loaded us into railroad cars for our trip across Germany and France, I got a kick out of the fact we were traveling in the same old cars I remembered hearing about from World War I. These were the old faurti et huit, or "forty and eight" cars designated to hold forty men or eight horses — and I'm sure horses wouldn't have enjoyed the miserable ride any more than we did.

It took us the better part of a week to get from Central Germany to the north coast of France, a short distance that seemed like forever as we traveled on the Army's "Great Circle Route."

But we couldn't complain too much after what many of us had been through. At least no one was shooting at us, and at mealtimes the train would stop at a siding and the cooks would whip out the portable stoves and cooking pots and prepare us a hot meal. This would take a few hours as everyone ate and goofed around, then we would all get back into our "horse cars" and chug on down the track at a snail's pace.

So you might say we were like one huge picnic. A truly "moveable feast," as we ambled our way through the countryside. And I suppose in some weird way we enjoyed it, knowing we were headed in the right direction at least. But if I was a travel agent, this little journey wouldn't appear among my packaged tours.

As we rumbled along, sniffing the air and commenting on the towns, villages and countryside, one thing remains vivid in my memory: the Germans were already busy repairing their homes and other buildings, though hostilities had barely ceased. They repaired as if war was a ho-hum business and they were merely getting ready for the next round.

In France it was a different story. We guessed, and were correct as it turned out, that the French were waiting to rebuild so they could be reimbursed for war damages by the United States. The Germans knew they had little choice but to get their own asses in gear.

We arrived in Le Havre, on the English Channel, and found a tent city waiting for us. After living and smelling like horses for a week, we were thrilled to have showers, good chow and cots to sleep on.

While in Le Havre we confronted one of the more ironic quirks of the military bureaucracy. We ran into men from another front-line unit that had been released to return home six weeks earlier. During World War II, you received so many points toward discharge for active service: one point a month for stateside service, two points for service overseas and bonus points for decorations.

Since they had spent time in England preparing for D-Day, while we trained in the States, these men probably had ten or so points more than the rest of us. These battle weary men were promised a "dearly wished quick trip home," but found that all transportation to the States was over booked. We, on the other hand were quickly loaded since we were headed for Japan. (Back in the States several weeks later, we learned that these poor guys were still hanging around Le Havre. Meanwhile the Japanese, having taken two A-bomb hits at Hiroshima and Nagasaki, had surrendered and we were being processed for discharge.)

The trip home was a pleasant one. We were loaded aboard a U.S. Navy troopship at Le Havre carrying our duffel bags and precious war souvenirs. Unlike the grim British ship transport that had brought us over the year before, the American ship was clean and orderly, and the bunks wonderful to men who had been sleeping on the ground and in half-destroyed barns and houses for many months.

Some of the guys took four or five showers a day, as if trying to wash away all their memories of war, and we gorged ourselves on the good and plentiful Navy chow while the Navy mess cooks, knowing what we'd been through, encouraged us and looked on approvingly.

(With all due respect to the British, their food reflected the bad time they were having of it, and, certainly, their lack of understanding of American tastes in food.)

Except for a typical Atlantic Ocean storm, which lasted three days, turning many of us horrible shades of green and yellow, our crossing was uneventful and landed us safely in New Jersey.

At this time there were still plans to invade Japan, however, and when we arrived in the States we were given home leave, but with the knowledge we would be returning to begin training for combat in the Pacific.

Then, to my unexpected delight, I was separated from my company and told I had accumulated enough points for discharge from the Army. By this time there was a lot of confusion over developments in the Pacific War (most likely because of the atomic bomb), so I was given temporary orders and sent to Ogden, Utah, of all places, to guard German POWs and await the outcome of the war.

This was a real goof-off job, compared to what I was use to. The camp was about four miles from Ogden, which is in a beautiful setting with mountains all around, and I was given a rifle and told to keep an eye on about thirty prisoners who were working in a local cannery.

With thirty guys to guard, I didn't know what I'd do if they decided to run. I don't even think the rifle was loaded. But I figured, where in the hell would they go? It seemed they had a pretty sweet deal where they were. As I quickly found out.

Instead of guarding prisoners, I was encouraged by the cannery foreman to do like the rest of the guards and hang up my rifle, join the work force and make a little money, which I could use since I would soon be a civilian.

Having improved my language skills considerably, I got along great with the Germans, who had learned considerable English as well. They laughed when I asked if they ever thought about running away. "Hell no!" said one blonde veteran of the Afrika Korps, "I am getting better food, good housing and more money than was ever paid by Rommel. We are getting cash pay," he explained, "each day when the shift is over. Is sehr gut, Ya?" he added, and I had to agree.

One day, an older veteran of the Wehrmacht whom I got to know, came up to me grinning and asked pleasantly, "So, Harold, tell me. How are things at home? We haven't been there for a while, you know. Did you leave anything standing?"

CHAPTER EIGHTEEN

Dorothy

I was still in the Army and stationed at Ogden when my wife Dorothy and I were married on September 11, 1945. We met for the first time when I visited my father Martin and stepmother a month earlier at their new home in Salem, Oregon. Dorothy and my stepmother Nell had met while working in the same Army hospital unit at Ft. Lewis, and she was visiting while I was on leave. We spent three great days getting acquainted, visiting the nearby sights in Oregon, and enjoying my folks' great hospitality. We fell in love and she decided to visit me when I returned to Utah, which I had suggested.

When I met her at the station in Ogden, I saw the look in her eyes, and she it in mine, and we both knew this was it. We were deeply in love and wanted to get married as soon as possible. My buddies were all for it. Since they had little to do but hang around waiting for discharge, they planned a big wedding before the post chaplain and an elaborate reception.

Unfortunately as we were filling out our marriage license, the clerk asked if we wanted to get married there or did we have other plans. Again, I looked at Dorothy, she looked at me, and we both said to hell with it and let the Justice of the Peace marry us right there.

The guys were mad as hell, of course, but they got over it. We spent our first honeymoon night in town, then moved onto the base for a glorious week in the camp's hospitality house before Dorothy went off to Illinois to visit her family.

Afterwards, she would move her things to Portland, Oregon, where we decided to live. I spent some time in Portland visiting my brother in 1943 before I went to war. I loved the city, which to this day, is still beautiful.

The Army sent me to Fort Lewis, Washington, for discharge. Since Portland is just down the road, I was a civilian with a new apartment by the time Dorothy arrived from Illinois.

When we calmed down from our reunion, I said to Dorothy the next morning, "Pack my lunch, I'm going to work."

"What do you mean, 'I'm going to work?' You don't even have a job!"

"Hey listen. You just pack my lunch pail and I'll have a job by tonight," I promised with pretty strong confidence for a farm boy who had no idea of where to find work in a big city.

As it turned out, I got a job that very morning at a downtown Portland parking garage and combination tuneup facility, and by evening returned home with an empty lunch pail and a full sense of accomplishment.

This year, 1997, Dorothy and I will have been married for 52 years, having so far shared a loving, long, full and interesting life. We have two children and six grandchildren.

My career has been varied and interesting as well, having been in quite a few different businesses. We operated two different restaurants in South Dakota, one in Mission, in the heart of the Rosebud Indian Reservation, the other in the beautiful Black Hills.

After some time, Oregon beckoned, so we moved to Salem. After a few odd jobs, I opened a television repair business. Later I purchased some land to raise registered Angus cattle. Then we added some large chicken houses, starting an egg business from a flock of 20,000 chickens. This started us on a program of raising pullets for other chicken farmers — which grew into a business of raising 150,000 pullets a year.

Sadly, however, Dorothy has in recent years been afflicted with Altzheimer's Disease, a cruel illness that steals the soul and spirit, and which has transformed our life into a day-to-day battle for survival.

Now I miss Dorothy even when we are together; having lost the lovely woman that shared my life for so many years. I have only memories now, but these are good ones. And some of the best are of those times when we traveled to Europe and visited old battlefields where I arrived as a boy and became a man.

Though the war ended decades ago, remnants can still be found everywhere, cruelly prodding our memories and defying time. Dorothy was always interested, having heard what I went through, and wanted to see where I had fought my war.

Yet on our last trip to Europe, curiously, I had a strange feeling of detachment. While Dorothy (was she sick now?) and I were walking among the war's debris, our heads down and looking for familiar pieces, I realized suddenly, I no longer wanted to seek out death's reminders.

I had had enough. The war was over for me forever.

Harold W. Knittel, Private First Class

BRONZE STAR AWARDS

Awarded for heroic service

PURPLE HEART AWARD

Awarded for sustaining a wound from enemy action

COMBAT INFANTRY BADGE

Awarded for operations in contact with the enemy.

PURPLE HEART RIBBON

To wear on uniform when you don't wear the actual award.

EUROPEAN, AFRICAN, CENTRAL EUROPE MEDAL

Three stars: Rhineland, Ardennes, Central Europe

AMERICAN SERVICE MEDAL

PURPLE HEART RIBBON

PRESIDENTIAL CITATION AWARD

12th Infantry awarded for excellence in Battle of Bulge

BOOK **90** PAGE **248**

10757

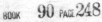

Army of the United States

Honorable Discharge

This is to certify that

HAROLD W KNITTEL   37 074 228   PRIVATE FIRST CLASS

HQ CO 1ST BN 12TH INF

Army of the United States

is hereby Honorably Discharged from the military service of the United States of America.

This certificate is awarded as a testimonial of Honest and Faithful Service to this country.

Given at   SEPARATION CENTER
FORT LEWIS WASHINGTON

Date   29 SEPTEMBER 1945

State of South Dakota, } ss   OFFICE OF
County of _____ }   REGISTER OF DEEDS

I hereby certify that the within instrument
was filed in this office for record on the
8th day of **Mar** A. D. **1949**
at **8:00** o'clock **9** M. and was duly
recorded in Book **2** _____ Discharge
Record _____ on Page **16**

Don W Hanlen
Register of Deeds.

By _____
Deputy.

Harvey D. Taylor
HARVEY D TAYLOR
LIEUTENANT COLONEL CAVALRY

ENLISTED RECORD AND REPORT OF SEPARATION
HONORABLE DISCHARGE

BOOK **90** PAGE **249**

1. LAST NAME - FIRST NAME - MIDDLE INITIAL	2. ARMY SERIAL NO.	3. GRADE	4. ARM OR SERVICE	5. COMPONENT
KNITTEL HAROLD W	37 074 228	PFC	INF	AUS

6. ORGANIZATION	7. DATE OF SEPARATION	8. PLACE OF SEPARATION
HQ CO 1ST BN 12TH INF	29 SEP 45	SEPARATION CENTER FORT LEWIS WASHINGTON

9. PERMANENT ADDRESS FOR MAILING PURPOSES	10. DATE OF BIRTH	11. PLACE OF BIRTH
105 RIVER ST SALEM OREGON	6 APR 19	JORDON S DAK

12. ADDRESS FROM WHICH EMPLOYMENT WILL BE SOUGHT	13. COLOR EYES	14. COLOR HAIR	15. HEIGHT	16. WEIGHT	17. NO. DEPEND.
SEE 9	BLUE	BROWN	5'7"	144 LBS.	1

18. RACE		19. MARITAL STATUS	20. U.S. CITIZEN	21. CIVILIAN OCCUPATION AND NO.
WHITE X / NEGRO / OTHER (specify)	SINGLE / MARRIED X / OTHER (specify)	YES / NO X	TRUCK DRIVER LIGHT

MILITARY HISTORY

22. DATE OF INDUCTION	23. DATE OF ENLISTMENT	24. DATE OF ENTRY INTO ACTIVE SERVICE	25. PLACE OF ENTRY INTO SERVICE
17 SEP 41		17 SEP 41	FT CROOK NEBR

26. REGISTERED	27. LOCAL S.S. BOARD NO.	28. COUNTY AND STATE	29. HOME ADDRESS AT TIME OF ENTRY INTO SERVICE
SELECTIVE SERVICE DATA — YES X / NO	1	TODD S DAK	RAPID CITY S DAK

30. MILITARY OCCUPATIONAL SPECIALTY AND NO.	31. MILITARY QUALIFICATION AND DATE (i.e., infantry, aviation and marksmanship badges, etc.)
LINEMAN TELEPHONE & TELEGRAPH 238	MARKSMAN M-1 RIFLE COMBAT INFANTRYMAN BADGE

32. BATTLES AND CAMPAIGNS

RHINELAND ARDENNES CENTRAL EUROPE GO 33 WD 45

33. DECORATIONS AND CITATIONS

AMERICAN DEFENSE SERVICE MEDAL PURPLE HEART GO 25 HQ 4TH INF 45 EUROPEAN AFRICAN MIDDLE EASTERN SERVICE MEDAL GOOD CONDUCT MEDAL BRONZE SERVICE STAR GO 38 HQ 4TH INF 45

34. WOUNDS RECEIVED IN ACTION

EUROPEAN 4 MARCH 45

35. LATEST IMMUNIZATION DATES				36. SERVICE OUTSIDE CONTINENTAL U.S. AND RETURN		
SMALLPOX	TYPHOID	TETANUS	OTHER (specify) TYPHUS	DATE OF DEPARTURE	DESTINATION	DATE OF ARRIVAL
1-25-44	6-25-44	6-28-44	12-15-44	11 SEP 44	EUROPEAN	19 SEP 44
					U S	12 JUL 45

37. TOTAL LENGTH OF SERVICE				38. HIGHEST GRADE HELD
CONTINENTAL SERVICE		FOREIGN SERVICE		TEC 5
YEARS	MONTHS	DAYS	YEARS	MONTHS	DAYS
3	2	21	0	10	2	

39. PRIOR SERVICE

NONE

10757

40. REASON AND AUTHORITY FOR SEPARATION

CONVENIENCE OF GOVERNMENT RR 1-1 (DEMOBILIZATION) AR 615-365 15 DEC 44

41. SERVICE SCHOOLS ATTENDED	42. EDUCATION (Years)
NONE	Grammar / High School 2½ / College

PAY DATA

43. LONGEVITY FOR PAY PURPOSES			44. MUSTERING OUT PAY		45. SOLDIER DEPOSIT	46. TRAVEL PAY	47. TOTAL AMOUNT, NAME OF DISBURSING OFFICER
YEARS	MONTHS	DAYS	TOTAL	THIS PAYMENT			
4	0	23	$ 300	$ 100	none	$ 85-45	220.78 E W WOHLGEMUTH

CAPT FD

INSURANCE NOTICE

IMPORTANT: IF PREMIUM IS NOT PAID WHEN DUE OR WITHIN THIRTY-ONE DAYS THEREAFTER, INSURANCE WILL LAPSE. MAKE CHECKS OR MONEY ORDERS PAYABLE TO THE TREASURER OF THE U.S. AND FORWARD TO COLLECTIONS SUBDIVISION, VETERANS ADMINISTRATION, WASHINGTON 25, D.C.

48. KIND OF INSURANCE	49. HOW PAID	50. Effective Date of Allotment Discontinuance	51. Date of Next Premium Due	52. PREMIUM DUE EACH MONTH	53. INTENTION OF VETERAN TO
Nat. Serv. / U.S. Govt. X / None	Allotment X / Direct to V.A.	30 SEP 45	(One month after SD) 31st OCT 45	$ 6 65	Continue X / Continue Only / Discontinue

54.

RIGHT THUMB PRINT

LAPEL BUTTON ISSUED ASR (2 SEP 45) 83

55. REMARKS (This space for completion of above items or entry of other items specified in W. D. Directives)

FOR CONVENIENCE, A CERTIFICATE OF ELIGIBILITY NO. 714323 HAS BEEN ISSUED BY THE VETERANS ADMINISTRATION TO BE USED FOR THE FUTURE REQUEST OF ANY GUARANTY OR INSURANCE BENEFIT UNDER TITLE III OF THE SERVICEMEN'S READJUSTMENT ACT OF 1944, AS AMENDED, THAT MAY BE AVAILABLE TO THE PERSON TO WHOM THIS SEPARATION PAPER WAS ISSUED.

56. SIGNATURE OF PERSON BEING SEPARATED	57. PERSONNEL OFFICER (Type name, grade and organization—signature)
Harold W. Knittel	JOHN J TAGGART MAJ AGD John J Taggart

WD AGO FORM 53-55
1 November 1944

This form supersedes all previous editions of WD AGO Forms 53 and 55 for enlisted persons entitled to an Honorable Discharge, which will not be used after receipt of this revision.

South Dakota Veterans WW II Bonus applied for.

Dorothy and Harold Knittel

My wife, Dorothy, was my main inspiration for writing this book. It was at her urging that we made our first trip back to Germany and Belgium after the war. She was highly interested and awed by the war remnants that were still visible. Her desire to hear my tales of the battles and the people I encountered, helped me realized I might have a story that would interest others.

-Harold Knittel

This book is dedicated to my family who
supported me in my endeavor.

I especially want to acknowledge my daughter Patty
who was instrumental in putting the book together.
She typed and organized the photos —
and mostly, she encouraged me to go on.

I also want to thank my sister Doris
who insisted I had a story worth telling.
Without her encouragement, I would not have
shared my thoughts and experiences with others.

All pictures and photographs in this document are courtesy of
Col. Gerden F. Johnson, author of *The History of the Twelfth Inf.
Regiment*, by arrangement from his wife, Emily L. Johnson.
Col. Gerden F. Johnson is now deceased.